Walking With My Angels

Walking With My Angels

A True Story

Keith Leon S.

About the Author Photo
Christina Stuart (Christina Stuart Photography)

Back Cover Photo
Alex Lowy (Alex Lowy's Photography Studio)

ISBN: 978-1-945446-75-7

This book is dedicated to my earthbound angel.
Thank you for every moment you spent with me.
You cracked my heart and belief system wide open.
You took me to do all the things I didn't get to do as a fatherless child.
You had patience with me, loved me unconditionally, and encouraged me.
Words will never be enough to express my thanks.

Praise for
Walking With My Angels

"*Walking With My Angels* is a vulnerable, honest, and inspiring story of how and why angels show up for us in our everyday lives."

—Bob Proctor, Author, Speaker and Featured Teacher from *The Secret*

"A self-help book that reads like a novel. I love this book."

—Marci Shimoff, #1 New York Times Bestselling Author of *Happy For No Reason* and Featured Teacher in *The Secret*

"A touching story that shows how we all can be guided to a better future with the help of our heavenly supporters, no matter our age or background."

—Seann Levine, High School Student

"*Walking With My Angels* is funny, spiritual, enlightening, and engaging. It's transparently written not only to inspire and guide you, but to help you remember and embrace those unexplainable experiences you had growing up but didn't understand or felt you had to hide. In this book, Keith shows us so beautifully that we are never alone. If you weren't aware of your angels before reading this, you will be after. Such an uplifting read!

—Lisa Winston, International Bestselling Author, TV Host, Producer, and Inspirational Speaker

"If you have ever wondered if angels are real or fiction, this book will help you decide."

—Adam Markel, International Bestselling Author of *Pivot: The Art & Science of Reinventing Your Career and Life*

"By reading this book, you'll earn your wings and the consciousness that will lift you above all your earthly concerns."

—Reverend Christian Sorensen, International Speaker, Transformational Leader, and Author of *Living from the Mountain Top: Be the Mystic You Were Born to Be*

"When light workers like Keith Leon S. follow their divine path to help others, it's clear that angels truly will support your journey. *Walking With My Angels: A True Story* shares many stories, revealing how angels helped him fulfill his purpose. The best part is this book will teach you how angels will help you do the same."

—Robert Clancy, #1 International Bestselling Author of *Soul Cyphers,* Spiritual Teacher and Co-Host of *The Mindset Reset Show*

"Thank God angels stepped in to save Keith's life, so he could step into his life purpose. I've known Keith for twenty-four years, and I can tell you he's one of those few rare people who actually walks his talk. He truly demonstrates what he teaches. The work he's here to do will help millions of people make contact with their heavenly helpers."

—Lin Van Gelder, Realtor

"I am so happy that *Walking With My Angels* is finally here! I've known Keith for many years, and it was a long wait until the angels told him it was time to write and release it. This book will make a difference in your life!"

—Ari Gronich, Bestselling Author, Speaker & Founder of Performance Therapy Academy

"With all the drama in Keith's life growing up, it's amazing that he has kept a positive outlook. What he has overcome is breathtaking, and it's amazing how he took those circumstances and used them for his good, and for the good of humankind."

—Shannon Gronich, Event Producer, Author, and Publicity Expert

"With practice, we can all feel and even see our angels. Keith's book easily helps you connect; you will feel your energy shift by simply looking at the cover."

—Swami S. Tirtha, Bestselling Author, Speaker and TV Host/Producer of *Talking With Our Angels TV Show*

"Keith Leon S. is truly a difference maker on this planet. *Walking With My Angels* is his life story that shares how angels have made a difference in his life, how they can make a difference in yours, and reunite you with the peace within."

—Lee Travathan, Celebrity Coach for Artists, Entertainers, Writers, Sports Figures, and Author of *The Rebel Writers* Book Series

"*Walking With My Angels* will take you on a journey. You'll feel each and every human emotion while reading this well told true story. You'll come out on the other side changed forever."

—Quinn Alexander Fontaine, Transformational Speaker, Comedian, and Bestselling Author of *Hung Like a Seahorse*

"A heart-felt, wise, honest, and tender book. We don't always get to choose what happens in this life, but we can choose to grow in compassion and wisdom as a result. *Walking With My Angels* makes accessible to the reader author Keith Leon's vulnerability. It's encouraging to read a book from such a solid and successful businessman talking about heavenly helpers."

—Debbi Dachinger, Syndicated Podcast Host, International Bestselling Author, and Visibility Media Strategist

"I hope this book is made into a movie. I am still astounded and in awe of this remarkable story!"

—Mark Hattas, Author, Speaker, and Entrepreneur, including Co-Founder of Journey's Dream

"If ever there was a time for a book that connects people with their inner guides, it's now. This book has come with perfect timing into your hands."

—Nancy Matthews, Speaker, Author,
and Co-Founder of Women's Prosperity Network

"Keith is just a regular guy who experienced supernatural circumstances. What he did with the knowledge he received will make a difference on this planet."

—Danielle Martins, Strategic Life Mentor/Coach,
Motivational Speaker and Co-author of the International
Bestseller, *Rising Up from Mental Slavery*

"I am pleased that Keith finally got to write this book. His story will expand the way you view angels. He has a different take on angels, and their purpose, than any other angel person out there."

—David Boufford, Founder, MrPositive.com

"*Walking With My Angels* is a book about tragedy, fear, bravery, and perseverance. If you are open to receiving it, there is healing grace within its pages (and beyond) to transform the landscape of your life."

—Christine Powers, Award-Winning International Soprano,
Founder of the Philosophers Camp

"I am glad to know that angels have my back. I knew all my life they existed, but I ignored them. Thanks to Keith for encouraging me to invite them into my everyday life."

—Daniel Gutierrez, Multiple Bestselling Author,
International Speaker, and Mindful Leadership Expert

"*Walking With My Angels* will be a game changer in your life. Make sure you read this book and pick up a copy for someone you love."

—A.J. Ali, Director and Producer of the film,
WALKING WHILE BLACK: L.O.V.E. Is The Answer

"I guarantee you've never read a book like this one. I can feel the energy coming off this book."

—Melissa Hitchcock, Dedicated Mother and Artist

"*Walking With My Angels* is not like any other angel book I've read before. This book will change your perspective and life as you know it! Angels are among us."

—Frances Castelli, Dedicated Mother and Author of the Bestselling Book, *The Kitchen Alchemist: How I Became My Own Food Scientist So My Kids Could Thrive With Anaphylactic Food Allergies*

"Keith's engaging style of writing and the content in this book make what some might think as impossible, real: bringing angels down to earth through his stories and practical application of how we are all supported by these beautiful beings of light."

—Abby Gooch, Intuitive Success Coach, Author, Speaker

"Holy crap, this book changed my life! Angels aren't just with other people, they're with me too!"

—Lucas J. Robak, Wellness Leader, Bestselling Author, and Authorpreneur Consultant

"I am inspired and excited to contact my angels because of Keith's message. This book will transform your connection with your inner guides."

—Tasha Chen, Transformational Speaker and Founder of Science of Getting Rich Academy

"I am inspired by the story Keith vulnerably shares in this book. His message will bring you to the awareness that you are and always have been enough, and you truly make a difference in this world."

—Melanie Colley, Real Estate Broker and Agent

"If you're looking to read something that will change your life forever, this is the book for you."

—Berny Dohrmann, Co-Founder of CEO Space,
International Speaker and Author of
Redemption: The Cooperation Revolution

"This book will make a difference in the world! Many lives will be forever changed from reading it."

—Charmaine Hammond, Motivational Speaker and
Bestselling Author of *On Toby's Terms*

"Stunning work. This book drew me in immediately and kept me in a state of awe and appreciation. If you've ever wondered if angels really exist, this book will answer the question for you."

—Karen McGregor, Bestselling Author, International Speaker,
and Founder of the Speaker Success Formula

"Keep in mind that the author of this book is a father, a husband, and a successful business man. He didn't seek out to be an angel guy, the angels found him, and made him their messenger."

—Gary Gregory, Husband, Father, and Motivational Leader

Contents

Part IV
The Path to Living My Purpose

Foreword

I've known Keith Leon S. for more than thirteen years, and it has always been clear to me that his purpose is to deeply and positively touch the lives of anyone and everyone he meets. He sings, he is a transformational speaker, and a bestselling author. It doesn't take long in his presence to be clear that no matter the circumstance, he always has your best interest in mind.

I've seen him go from first time author with minimal success to an international bestselling author of multiple titles. I've watched his business grow by leaps and bounds into a full-service publishing company that helps people move their stories, ideas, their mission, and their message out into the world. I have enjoyed watching him grow his business and his career while continuing to be a heart-centered, loving, and caring man.

Now Keith has written a beautiful book—*Walking with My Angels*—his life story, including how his angels saved his life on many occasions. In this book, he makes suggestions for how to contact your angels.

Keith also introduces a new definition of the words, *earthbound angel,* and he shares in detail how an angel came to him in the flesh and spent time teaching him to be a believer in more than what can be seen with the eyes. This earthbound angel worked with Keith to ready him for his destiny here on Earth. The angel put Keith on his path, facilitated an out-of-body experience that revealed Keith's life purpose, and then literally saved his life before moving on to help the next person.

This book will inspire you to open your heart to all possibilities. If you don't believe in angels now, you may before you complete this book. If you do believe in angels, miracles might happen with the knowledge you'll gain. Who knows? There are no accidents. You have this book in your hands right now for a reason. I know that reading it will transform your life.

May your life be filled with the light and love you deserve.

Jack Canfield, Co-creator of
Chicken Soup for the Soul® and author of
The Success Principles™: How to Get from Where You Are to Where You Want to Be

Acknowledgments

To my incredible wife, business partner, and best friend, Maura Leon S. I love you so much. You are patient, kind, loving, understanding, forgiving, smart, talented, and beautiful. Thank you for saying yes to our destiny together, and for walking side by side with me through all it has taken to get to this point in my life.

To Aaron and Timar Smith. I could not be prouder of you two, and of how loving you are to me and to others.

To my dad and second mom Nita. Dad, I am so happy you came back into my life. I enjoyed getting to know you, swapping stories, and catching up on lost time. Nita, thank you for being insistent that Dad pick up the phone and call me so that we could build a great relationship.

To my other mom and dad, Rita and Herb Di Gioia. Thank you for giving birth to such a wonderful daughter and for accepting me into your loving family. You've been so supportive of me and my work. It's much appreciated.

My love and appreciation to my family members, Aunt Carol, David Smith, Crystal Smith, Melissa Smith, Diana Di Gioia, Melody Masi, Dante Di Gioia, Maria Di Gioia, David Di Gioia, Larinda Di Gioia, Heidi Prentice, Robyn Easley-Johnson, Jerome and Mason Johnson, Bryan Wiersma, Deanna Wiersma, and Will Wiersma. Thanks for the love and support.

To my mentors and father figures, Ben Cuny, Russell Smith Sr., Jack Canfield, Bob Proctor, Adam Markel, John Rosas, and Donna-Lisa Valencia. You inspired me to face every seeming obstacle, boldly and bravely. You've been an example of what grace, leadership, strength, honesty, and vulnerability look like.

Thank you to all the participants in the *Who Do You Think You Are?* book. You were all part of my first major success. Thanks to the few who took me under their wing, and taught me about the business of books and how to create a bestseller.

To the Agape choir and community. I miss you and I thank God for you. I am so grateful for live streaming—when I get homesick, I can always listen to a service, close my eyes, take a deep breath, and I am right back in the room with you. There is only one Agape!

To my dear friends who've rooted me on, encouraged me, and believed in me all along: Rudy Milanovich, Nida Palpallatoc, Wayne Bottomley, Heather Marsh, David Boufford, Les Demarco, Joseph L. Seoane, Jessica Brace, Ari Gronich, Shannon Burnette-Gronich, Robbie Brooks Moore, Kevin Moore, Cheri Camp, Amy Todisco, Dave Hartshorn, Edie Connolly, Bill Carnright, Angela Cormier, Cameron Love, Alison J. Kay, Nioshi Jackson, Chris Gray, Stuart Grossman, Erik Peterson, Melissa Hitchcock, Susan Picking, Mike Wheeler, Ron, Jamie and Justin Malvin, The Recla's, Cynthia Schwartzberg, Heather Rienhardt, Aubry Tager, Dr. Kevin Poulston, Dr. Bob Levine, Charlene Levine, Mary Raymakers, Scot and Patricia Ferrell, Mike and Bradlee Snow, Sammy and Audrey Ellis Pyon, Kat Wells, Morgana Starr, Daena Dussich, Mark Hattas, Lucas Robak, Tasha Chen, EBC members, Seann Levine, Rev. Christian Sorensen, Quinn Alexander Fontaine, Debbi Dachinger, Nancy Matthews, Danielle Martins, Katerina Cozias, Christine Powers, Daniel Gutierrez, Frances Castelli, Abby Gooch, Melanie Colley, Karen McGregor, Gary Gregory, Ben Adams, David Burchall, Maribel Jimenez, and Amareena Wildflower, Rebecca Kirstein, Zach Lush, Trish Matthews, Sammy Bindell, Jason D. Mitchell, Tonijean Amato Kulpinski, Lynn Rose, Terri Levine, Marjean Holden, Craig Shoemaker, John Rozenberg, Kelly Corsino, Edith Connellee, Sonya

P. Nagy, Debra Halperin Poneman, Ken Rochon, and Helice Sparky Bridges.

Thank you so much to those who have given me inspiration to follow my path: Doreen Virtue, Norma Milanovich, Esther Hicks (Teachings of Abraham), Terri Cole Whittaker, Reverend Michael Bernard Beckwith, Rickie Byars Beckwith, Robert Clancy, Lorna Byrne, James Van Praugh, Dannion Brinkley, Brian L. Weiss, MD, Marci Shimoff, Lisa Winston, Robert Clancy, Lin Van Gelder, Swami S. Tirtha, Lee Travathan, A.J. Ali, Berny Dohrmann, Charmaine Hammond, and Raymond Moody, MD.

Thank you to the angels both earth bound and ethereal who've helped me on my journey, including Anael, Anahel, Ariel, Ed Oakley, Gabrael, John, Larry, Metatron, Michael, Muriel, Raphael, Uriel, Wakeel, and Zachriel.

Many thanks to my favorite photographer, Christina Stuart (Christina Stuart Photography), for all the amazing photos you've taken for me.

Thank you to all the Indiegogo contributors. And special thanks to the following large donation sponsors: Jack the Cat: An Angel's Tale author, Bradlee Snow, Carlee Contreras, Christine Powers, Dr. Karen Kan, Fiz Anthony, and Chris Gray.

And special thanks to my book-creation team: Rona Gofstein, Heather Taylor, Peggy Gilbart, Karen Burton, Dot Brookes, Rudy Milanovich, Maryna Zhukova, and Autumn Carlton. You have done such a wonderful job helping me bring my story to print. I am forever grateful for your work on this book.

Introduction

You don't have to believe me.

You don't have to believe in angels.

But if you join me for this journey, no matter what you believe today, I guarantee you'll be thinking differently by the end.

This is a story about my life, and it's a story about angels. What you will read in this book is, to the best of my recollection, the absolute truth. While I have trouble keeping the timeline of what happened straight, the events themselves are crystal clear. My imagination has never been strong, but my recollections are vivid.

When people first hear my stories, sometimes they think I'm stretching the truth—until they spend some time with me. I completely understand. In many ways, my life resembles a blockbuster film. The lows are extremely low, the conflict is real and intense, and there's a mega-super happy ending. If you have doubts, keep reading—spend a little more time with me, and you will see the truth.

Over the years, I have discovered that there are two parts of me, and these two parts are in constant battle with each other.

First, there is the part that can manifest whatever I desire, at lightning speed, by doing nothing more than wishing, imagining, seeing it as done, and putting action behind it. This is the part of me that is helped by angels—lots and lots of angels—surrounding me, protecting me, and guiding me in each moment.

This side of me is the believer. When I allow myself to reside in that part of me, I know that dreams can come true. I understand that I am, in actuality, living a dream in each moment.

Then there's the other part of me, the part that is forever in doubt. This side considers the situation, starts to stand up, then pauses, and sits back down.

This part of me says things like:

Naaaaah. No way. Can't do it.

You may have a similar battle going on inside you. In this book, you'll read about the roles both these parts have played during my life, and how they have shaped who I am today. Most of the lessons I have learned in my life, as you will see, have involved a battle—or at least a negotiation—between these two sides of me.

I don't always learn a lesson the first time it is presented. Like you, I repeat mistakes. I know if I keep trying, eventually I'll get it. It's encouraging to see that the amount of time it takes before I learn a lesson is shorter, now, than it used to be.

All these lessons have been written into the distinctive—and beautiful—design of my path, which you will learn about as you read this book. Your life path has its own unique design. It is my hope that, by offering you some insight into my life, you will receive insight into your own.

Whether or not you currently believe in angels, when you finish this book, I trust you will. I would be overjoyed if this book helps you to become aware of the role of angels in your own life.

I know if it had not been for my guardian angel as a child, I would have been molested behind the corner church and would have died—in an auto accident, from being asphyxiated, in a fall over a cliff—and the list goes on. I should have been dead seven times already, but angels intervened to keep me here.

Angels have intervened for me over and over again. They have kept me from harm, have helped me find my path, and have given me a better life.

For years, I wondered:

What makes me so special that angels would go out of their way to save me?

What is my purpose that I should be spared when so many others are not?

The answers to these questions and more are within the pages of this book. As you read about my experiences, you will meet my guardian angels and earthbound angels. You will hear their voices and see how they shaped my story.

As you make your way through this book, it will become apparent to you that there was a plan for my life. There were people I needed to meet and people who needed to meet me. There were vital tasks I needed to accomplish for myself and for others—including the writing of this book.

Thirty years ago, I was shown my life's purpose. This *knowing* has been the inspiration for everything I have done as a speaker, a singer, a book mentor, and a publisher. Everything I have done in my life and in my business has been a preface for this book.

I was told I would write a book called *Walking with My Angels*.

I was told to wait for an angel voice to tell me when to begin.

I waited, and waited, and waited some more, as I went about my business living my purpose.

It was a long wait.

Not long ago, I was hiking in the beautiful mountains of Vermont with my dear friend, Amy Todisco, who happens to be a skilled life coach.

She asked me, "So, when are you going to write that angel book?"

I told her "When I get the call, so to speak. I was told I would be instructed when to write it. I've been waiting for twenty-nine years."

"Oh, okay. Well, I think it's a good time for it."

"Yeah, you and me both."

We continued to hike.

Then I heard a voice, from over my shoulder, say, loud and clear: *It's time.*

I replied silently: *It's time for the book?*

Yes, the book. It's time.

I stopped walking. Amy looked at me questioningly.

"Amy, I just heard the voice, and you were right—it *is* time to write the book. Thanks for asking that question. I've waited so long, anticipating this day. I'm so excited!"

Amy jumped immediately into coaching mode.

She said, "That's great. I am so excited for you. So, when will you start? Will you write daily or commit to a certain amount of hours per week? Will you set a date and time to begin?"

"As soon as I get home," I told her, "I will get my calendar out and schedule time to write. Thanks, coach!"

I started the book that day. As I sat down to create what I call the *roadmap* for this book, I realized how much time this project would take. My schedule was heavy with work assisting other authors, and as I looked at my calendar for time to write, I felt overwhelmed. I was already booked out a few months. It was frustrating not to be able to dive right in.

One day, my wife, Maura, said, "You are a marathon writer, Honey. You know you can get a lot done if you sit down and write for an extended time. When are you going to block out enough days to write your book?"

"I don't know. My schedule is completely full. I know it's time to write, but I don't want to cancel commitments, or shift things around. It's all feeling a bit daunting at the moment."

I left to run errands, and when I returned, Maura had my schedule book in her hands.

"It's done," she said. "I looked at what was scheduled already and found nine days that weren't booked yet. They're six weeks away, but the days are right here, in the schedule. Do you think you can write your book in nine days?"

"Wow, nine days?"

Because I had already written it repeatedly in my head, I was sure I could do it.

The heart of this book was written in those nine days. If you have ever written a book, you will be aware that this is incredibly fast. My hands typed at record speed as my angels assisted me, and it was a joy and a pleasure to write with them.

During those nine days, I remembered the stories I wanted to tell in sharp detail. I had vivid visions of conversations, remembering every word. It was like actually going back in time. It felt so good to experience all of it again—even the scarier times. It was a joy being taught again by my angels, and being reminded again of my purpose.

Looking back, I felt proud of all I had done to live into that purpose. Over the years, I have helped thousands of people to write their books, to elevate their mission and their message.

Now it is time for mine.

My suggestion, which comes from my own grateful heart, is that you read this book with an open heart and an open mind. This book is meant to uplift you, to raise your energy, and to take your awareness of yourself and your angel helpers to a higher level.

You have been assigned a guardian angel, whether you know it or not. If you pay attention, you will notice your angel helping you. Of course, you might not see this assistance as angelic—you might be calling it intuition, divine guidance, or inner knowing, and that's fine. Angels don't care what you call them as long as you listen and take action as they guide you. They are not in it for the glory or recognition.

Their main goal is to help ensure that you stay here for the time you are supposed to be here. There are so many moving parts in the course of a life, and angels are here to do what it takes to make sure you make it to your predetermined expiration date.

As you read this book and the stories within it, take time to reflect on your life and to *notice*. Notice the times when something happened to alter the path you were walking. These are probably some of the times when an angel has stepped in to help you.

Was there a time when you changed your routine or took another way home from work?

Have you ever had a feeling you shouldn't do something, and you altered your course because of that feeling?

Have you ever given a friend some remarkably sound advice and thought to yourself, "Where did that come from?"

Have you ever conquered a fear that was so great and strong that you were sure you received some otherworldly help or guidance?

Have you ever had a near death experience, and lived to tell the story?

It is likely that an angel has been by your side in these moments, lending a hand. They are there, all the time, making a difference in our lives. They are usually unnoticed, and receive no credit for all they do.

Angels are among us, and they take many forms. I once had an earthbound angel stay with me for over a year. He took me from not believing in anything to believing in everything, and, let me tell you, this was not an easy mission. He would show me a miracle on Monday, and I would have myself talked out of it by Tuesday. I used to call him Job because Lord knows he had the patience of that biblical man. His mission was to save me from myself. He succeeded. I would not be alive today if it were not for him.

This book tells the story of my journey, walking with these angels. My wish for you is that you enjoy every word. I hope the words in this book awaken something within you that perhaps you didn't know was there.

If you haven't been aware of angels in your life, I trust that you will be inspired to notice them. And that your eyes will be opened so you can recognize the many times in your life when angels have touched you, protected you, and helped you to make choices.

If you were already aware of your angels, you will be able to experience another level of understanding and connection after reading my story. This book, above all, is about ascension and awareness. There are no accidents. This book has landed in your hands at the perfect time and for the right reasons. Allow the process of your ascension to unfold in its perfect time in the most perfect way.

Please feel free to write to me and share what has become present to you and through you, while reading this book.

All the best, and enjoy the read.

PART I

It's All Preparation

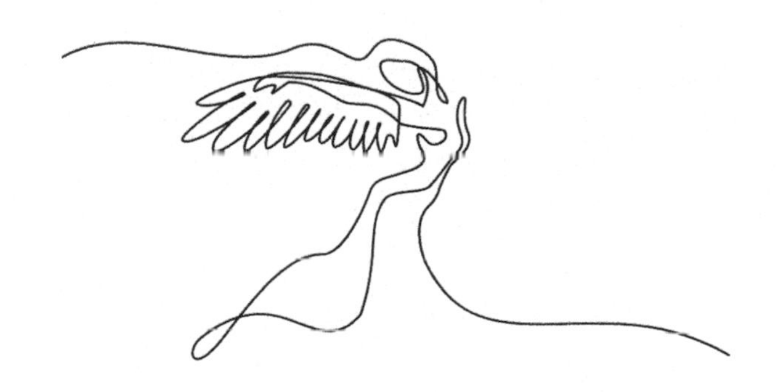

1

Growing Up
Mom, Mel, and Hearing My Guardian Angel

It's difficult to say exactly when angels started to grace my life.

When I consider my earliest childhood memories, it seems to me that I always could sense, feel, and hear an angel presence. As a child, I thought of him as my guardian angel.

I always knew where he was and could plainly hear his voice. Looking back, it's clear to me that my guardian angel protected me from harm and kept me out of trouble. My guardian angel gave me instructions—and I listened.

Did you ever sense such a presence when you were a child?

Think back on your early years. You may recall being aware of an angel or an undefined presence that gave you comfort or assistance. You may have to think very hard—it may only be a vague recollection now.

Children can see, sense, and hear many things adults cannot. This is a precious gift of childhood. Unfortunately, most parents dismiss children's insights completely. A child's angel connection is likely to be called an *imaginary friend.* A parent may even make a joke out of it, not appreciating that their child may be in contact with beings of light.

Sadly, the unsupported child will usually start to ignore the connection as well. This is a terrible loss, both for the child and for the adult they are to become.

If you have a child who speaks of angels, do your best to be positive, interested, and supportive. You may be fostering a practice that will be a life-long blessing for your child.

Like most parents, my mother dismissed my angel connection, although she was respectful of my feelings. I'm everlastingly thankful that, in spite of this, I was able to preserve my ability to listen to angels; they have been with me my whole life.

Beginnings

My childhood was challenging. However, I wasn't always an unhappy child. I don't think I dwelled on the challenges when I was living through them. I probably didn't complain any more than any other kid did; my life felt normal to me. Now, when I look back on my youth, I can clearly see all the dangers and difficulties on my path, and I feel lucky to have survived it. The angels were with me on my journey. I feel sure that I never would have made it out of childhood without them.

I was born in Norwalk, California, and I grew up in Long Beach, California. My parents divorced when I was two years old, and my sister, Tina, and I were raised in my mother's custody. I rarely saw my father, who moved to Virginia when I was seven. I can only recall spending one Christmas with him.

Parents can have an enormous impact on the person we turn out to be. The absence of my father probably changed me in significant ways. My mother, with whom I spent most of my childhood, has certainly affected the way I think and act. I am not much like her; in fact, I'm the polar opposite of my mother in many ways. Nonetheless, she helped shape the person I am.

She was troubled and ill, and her behavior was erratic. But despite my acute awareness of what she lacked as a parent, I have never overlooked the importance of what she *did* give me. My mother unfailingly modeled for me a vitally important quality that has deeply affected the course of my life.

That quality is love.

Even with the illnesses and setbacks she suffered over the course of decades, it was my mother who taught me to love unconditionally.

We lived in a little shack in Long Beach, California, just over the bridge from Compton. Mom did the best she could to provide for Tina and me, but it was a sparse existence. Her poor health meant that she didn't work. We lived on welfare. Food and clothes usually came from church members, with occasional contributions from my grandmother. There were more hard times than good, to be sure, but I played like any kid, and I had friends. I have some good memories of my childhood that make me smile when I look back.

My mother was manic-depressive, given to frequent periods of low energy alternating with bizarre periods of manic energy. In addition, she was agoraphobic and claustrophobic. For years, her condition was further complicated by poor health and obesity. I remember her lying in bed, crying, for long periods. And, although she taught me how to love, she did not offer a lot of parenting.

For my older sister, Tina, it was an especially challenging childhood. She and my mother, both strong-willed, fought constantly when my mother had the energy. When my mother was in her extended depressed periods, she was absent and unresponsive. For long stretches of time, Tina—only a young teenager herself—took care of me completely. Looking back, I imagine it must have been very hard for her. All that time, she probably wanted to be having fun, like the other teenagers, but instead, she had to be responsible for our home and for me.

For many years, Tina played all the adult roles in my life. She was my sister, my mother, and my father—as well as my bodyguard. Once, a guy smacked both of my ears, costing me my hearing for several hours. In front of a group of his friends, she kicked that guy's ass. Needless to say, none of those kids ever messed with me again.

Considering her age and the challenges of our situation, I think Tina did a fantastic job helping raise me. Circumstances made us close as kids. Love, respect, and understanding made us close for life. Although I wasn't aware of it at the time, I have no doubt that angels worked through her to help us get through those difficult years.

As you might imagine, we didn't develop healthy social skills in our home. Communication in our family was piss-poor at best. The same was true for conflict resolution. The lack of these skills hindered me for a good portion of my early life. Because of this, I understand their importance better than most people do. I have spent a great deal of energy trying to learn and improve these skills as an adult.

None of us knew how to express feelings in a healthy way. Generally, we would hold in our feelings for as long as possible, and then explode, saying mean and hateful things. After one of these exchanges, someone would storm out of the house, slamming the door behind them. I learned this pattern and it caused problems in my adult relationships.

Adventures with My Mother

Manic periods with my mother were brief compared with her periods of depression, but they involved memorable adventures for Tina and me.

Living with a manic-depressive parent meant that Tina and I never knew what to expect. My mother's moods changed dramatically, without warning. She could be sad and withdrawn, or unreasonably angry, or giddy with happiness. She could be warm and gentle. She could be outrageously funny. Her unpredictability led to a life of excitement for me.

I remember being woken up in the middle of the night to my mother's voice calling me by my pet name, "Son-shine! Let's go cruising!"

On these nights, my sister and I would then be shuffled into our brown station wagon for some crazy escapade. As odd as they were, I enjoyed these nights. For a child, they were often great fun. In addition, they were the only times I felt like I had a mother.

My mother was full of energy during those times, and she was entertaining. She would take any dare offered to her. One evening, we were out cruising in a residential neighborhood and came to a round park filled with trees. My sister and I dared her to drive through the park, and she promptly did.

Once, a lady drove by us and yelled out of her window, "Where did you get your license?"

My mother yelled, "Cracker Jacks!"

It was one of the funniest moments of my childhood—to this day, it still makes me laugh.

My mother was reckless and, as I have said, unpredictable. The manic outings were exciting and sometimes dangerous—and some of my best memories of being with my mother. There were some late nights for us. I would sometimes try to tell her that I needed to get to sleep because I had school the next day. She would tell me not to worry; if I didn't feel like going to school in the morning, she would write me a note. She was unconcerned about me skipping school—setting me up to develop poor school habits that persisted for years.

In her manic phases, my mother was capable of anything. She was truly a loving person, and looking back, I think her manic expression of love was to try to make our most outrageous wishes come true. When my sister had a crush on Donny Osmond, for example, we went to the church the Osmond's attended so my sister could sit in the same room with her idol. I ended up in a Sunday school class with his little brother, Jimmy, who became a friend.

She drove to the Osmond's house multiple times, where we would park and wait in our car for a glimpse of Donny. One day, Mrs. Osmond came out to get the newspaper while we were in front of the house. When she saw our family sitting in the car, she graciously invited us in. My sister was in heaven; I was feeling both excited and embarrassed.

We were given a tour of their home and had a wonderful time visiting. It was great to feel more like friends and less like stalkers. Jimmy and I connected again, and I gave him a yo-yo shaped as a football. Years later I would see him play with that yo-yo on the Merv Griffin show. When Jimmy told Merv that a friend gave him the yo-yo, I felt so special to be spoken of that way.

Many of my most memorable childhood experiences were the result of a combination of my mother's good intentions and her manic behavior. Watching the Jerry Lewis Telethon one year, I told my mother one of my wishes—someday, I wanted to be one of the people answering phones and taking pledges at the telethon.

My mother smiled, and she started getting us ready to go.

She took us to the telethon location and bypassed the lines at the audience door. Walking confidently, she took us, instead, to a side door. Ignoring the security guard, she looked in and spotted Bert Convy inside.

She said, "Bert, darling, how have you been? It's been so long. How are the wife and kids?"

Bert looked a bit confused, but opened his arms to embrace her in a hug and proceeded to chat with her about his wife and kids.

He began to show us around. My mother and he chatted like old friends as we walked. I wondered what he was thinking.

Probably something like: *Damn, I don't remember who this lady is. Should I know her?*

To tell you the truth, even *I* wasn't sure—did my mother actually know him?

Bert showed us around backstage. As he did, I could see the celebrities answering the phones. My heart started to pound when I saw Susan Dey, my biggest crush at the time. I told my mother that I would love to sit next to her. She called Bert over and spoke briefly to him.

Bert walked me to the phones and said to Susan, "This young man will be joining you to answer the phones. If you could walk him through the process, it would be much appreciated."

My mother was a powerful force, as you can see. Her daring, unapologetic manner seemed to charm people into doing what she wanted.

She had already made two of my wishes come true that day. I was answering the phones *and* sitting with Susan Dey. Susan proceeded to teach me how to take a pledge. I sat there, next to my crush, answering phone calls and talking with Susan in between the calls. By the time her shift was up, we had connected well. When she was about to leave, I asked her if I could have a kiss. She blushed and gave me a peck on the cheek. I was in heaven!

My mother taught my sister and me how to approach celebrities. She told me never to call TV and movie stars by their character's name.

She said, "It puts them off, and that's no way to start a relationship."

She also taught me to make statements like: *I love your work.* She explained that talking this way invited a meaningful connection and would help the celebrity to see me as more of an admirer of their craft than a crazed fan.

However, when I met another idol of mine—Henry Winkler—in the parking lot that day, without thinking, I impulsively yelled out, "Fonzie!"

I was immediately embarrassed—after all, I knew better—but he kindly said, "Name's Henry Winkler. What's your name, young man?"

I told him and apologized for calling him Fonzie. Henry was forgiving and friendly. He asked me what I was doing there, where my mother was, and so on. I was on a break from answering phones at the time, and when he realized I was wandering around alone, I think he felt it was best to keep me with him until Mom found me herself. He kept chatting with me, and after what seemed like hours to me—it was probably about twenty minutes—my mother found me, apologized, and told me it was time to go back into the telethon.

He said, "No problem, ma'am. He's a good kid, and it was nice to meet him."

I waved to Henry as we walked off. I would never forget that experience.

I met many other stars that day, including Sugar Ray Robinson, Scatman Crothers, Mario Andretti, Rick Springfield, Jack Klugman, Cloris Leachman, Carol Channing, Bern Nadette Stanis, and Linda Blair. What a day it was for this little boy!

On the way home from our adventure, I excitedly recounted my time with *The Fonz*, Susan Dey, and the other celebrities. During that conversation, I asked my mom if she indeed knew Bert Convy, or if she had just made it up so we could get inside.

She said, "Son, if you walk into any room acting as if you own it, you will own it. If you act like you are supposed to be there, people will find a reason to invite you in."

As much as anything she ever said or did, those words have stayed with me, and they have helped me many times, both in my career and in my personal life.

Mel: Season of Joy and Heartbreak

As kids, Tina and I became accustomed to life with Mom and did our best to weather the ups and downs. Then, when I was eight years old, Mom met a man named Melvin Heward. He was an amazingly loving and tenderly sweet. I remember him being very tall. He was also someone I looked up to, admired, and trusted. Up to that point in time, I hadn't felt like that about anyone in my short life.

Mel and my mother met, fell in love, and were engaged in record time. He was very kind to my sister and me, and we looked forward to having a father figure around our house. Soon came the day that Mom and Mel married, and I was the ring bearer at their wedding. Mom seemed truly happy for the first time—at least as far as my sister and I could remember.

It was a time of joy for all of us. Sadly, it wouldn't last for long.

Five short days after the wedding, Mel died.

He was on his motorcycle, waiting for the streetlight to turn green. A drunk driver hit him from behind, throwing Mel and his motorcycle 90 feet. The driver then hit Mel again and dragged him another 250 feet. Mel was rushed to a hospital, and my mother arrived just in time to witness doctors and nurses, with paddles out, trying to revive him, as his heart had stopped beating. As much as they tried, they could not re-start his heart; the damage was too severe.

What a tragic and heartbreaking loss it was—for all of us. Many times since, I have wondered how different our lives would have been if Mel had only lived.

He was as close to Jesus as any man I ever met, a deeply good man of great strength and love. I swear that, if you squinted your eyes and opened your heart enough, you'd have seen a white light around his head. I'm grateful I had the chance to know him, even though he wasn't in my life for long. Some people are not meant to stay in this world, however much we want them to remain with us.

We were all grieving, but losing Mel put my mother into a tailspin. We thought we had seen her depressed before, but nothing we had ever witnessed could match the years after Mel's death. She would barely get out of the bed. The only time we'd see her up was to go to the bathroom. If you've seen the movie *What's Eating Gilbert Grape*, you have an idea of what my mother had become. She'd hold me in her arms and cry for hours on end. I loved her, but I didn't know how to help her, except to be there for her. For years she stayed in bed, sobbed, and re-lived her loss.

Much later, my mother and I had a conversation that helped me to understand the extent of her desperation at that time. As an adult, I had become aware that I had been saved from death, by angel intervention, a total of seven times. While talking to my mother about this, she asked me to tell her about the seven times. I discovered that I could only recall six.

"That's strange," I said. "I feel sure it was seven times, but hadn't really counted them until now."

She said, "I know what it was. There must be a part of you that has always known. I should tell you so you don't spend the rest of your life looking for number seven."

Then she told me a chilling story.

I learned that the first time my guardian angel saved me, he spoke to my mother, not to me.

Not long after Mel's death, my mother almost killed all of us. In her tailspin of depression, she became suicidal. She didn't want to live, but she couldn't die without us either. She decided she would end us all. First, she closed all the windows in the house, and closed our bedroom door while my sister Tina and I played in our room. Next, she turned on the gas and opened the stove.

As the house filled with the invisible lethal vapor, she clearly heard a voice say: *No, you can't do that!*

She looked around, but didn't see anyone.

Again, she heard: *No, you can't do that.*

She got spooked, went over to the stove, turned it off, opened the windows, and never mentioned it to anyone. She never considered doing this again.

She ended her story by saying, "Now I know it must have been your guardian angel that told me to stop. I heard his voice as plain as day. He told me, 'No, you can't do that' so I stopped. I'm so sorry. I'm so glad I didn't do it," and she wept.

I wept too. I cried for the pain she was in, and I cried in gratitude for the angel who had intervened.

The second time an angel saved me was also during the period after Mel's death.

Mel had been married and divorced before meeting my mother, and he had children from his first marriage. When I was about nine years old, my mother reached out to Mel's ex-wife. She was missing him so much she decided she wanted to get to know his family. We were invited to come meet her and Mel's children and spend time with them in Utah.

On the drive, my mother left my sister and me in the station wagon at a gas station. She left the car in neutral. The station was located on the edge of a huge cliff. As we waited for her, Tina and I felt the car begin to drift backwards, toward the cliff.

We started screaming. There was a guardrail at the cliff edge. The station wagon hit the rail and broke through, leaving us teetering on the brink. There was a very long drop to the rocks below. People were scrambling to help us.

It was terrifying. I remember being frozen in fear. It felt like one wrong move or one wrong breath would send us over the cliff.

Someone hooked a towline under the bumper, and a truck pulled us to safety. My mother, already impaired due to depression, was traumatized. She was able to continue the journey, however. Sometimes, my mother was amazingly resilient, considering the circumstances. We did make it to Utah, and spending time getting to know Mel's family was a treat.

My mother's depression persisted after we returned home. During this mourning period, small improvements in Mom's state of mind would be followed by relapses. As a child, over and over again, I would watch her get better by slow and tiny increments and then in one moment, would witness the erasure of all improvement. We did our best to take care of her, but, of course, Tina and I were not equipped to deal with her condition. We were children.

Even my television choices affected her. I remember we had to avoid any medical drama shows or scenes. I remember once watching an episode of *Emergency* in which a patient was rushed into the ER. As nurses and doctors worked on the patient, his heart stopped, and the paddles came out.

My mom freaked out, screaming, "Change the channel! Change the channel!"

I realized that it was the same scene she had witnessed at the hospital, right before Mel died. I ran to turn the channel while I watched her fall apart again; any emotional progress she had made was erased by that one scene on the television. I know now, looking back, that it wasn't my fault, but then, I felt terrible.

I closely monitored what we watched on TV after that. If I saw anyone being wheeled into an ER, I would fly across the room and turn that circular channel knob.

How did I manage during these extraordinarily difficult years?

My guardian angel never left my side. I could always feel his comforting and guiding presence. During these extended times of drama and fear, there were still moments of love and connection with my mother and sister.

Then, as now, it was my guardian angel who helped me to focus on those good moments, to draw them out and remember them, to hold onto them and let them carry me through the hard times.

Conversations with My Guardian Angel

Now that you know a bit about my childhood, you can better understand how precious my guardian angel was to me. Growing up in poverty meant spending my early years under poor living conditions in a bad neighborhood—the 'hood, as we referred to it—with inferior schools. These circumstances may sound awful, but they were probably easier to weather than the emotional difficulties we faced as children. The lack of a father figure, combined with my mother's mental and emotional disabilities, left us without adult care, guidance, comfort, and security.

My guardian angel filled in those gaps for me. I always felt bad that Tina didn't hear an angel like I did. I don't know why I was so blessed, and she wasn't. I do feel certain that she had a guardian looking out for her, even though she couldn't sense him.

The sound of my guardian angel's voice graced my childhood from the beginning. In my insecure world, he served as a protective force. He told me things that kept me out of harm's way, and he provided advice, comfort, and support. Because I spoke to him out loud, my mother knew about him from the beginning. Initially, she thought he was just an imaginary friend, but she never made me feel as though I wasn't speaking the truth when I told her things he said to me.

Looking back, I feel grateful to her for that. Her acceptance meant that I never had to pretend I wasn't talking to him, and this let him stay an active part of my life.

My angel and I had many conversations. It wasn't simply hearing a voice, although I could hear his voice as clearly as any other. We had back and forth dialogues. I always knew where the angel was by the sound of his voice. In the house, he was usually hanging out in a corner by the ceiling. Outside, he was on my right shoulder and his voice would sound like someone standing behind me just to the right.

He didn't appear with lightning and thunder or a bright light. I could just hear his voice and I could always feel his presence. His voice was deep, yet gentle and soothing, and he had a great laugh. He shared many things with me as I was growing up. If I had a question I didn't feel my mother or her friends could answer, I'd ask him. He was straightforward with me; he always told me the truth. It was one of the things I loved most about him.

The conversations were many, and the range of topics would probably surprise you.

If you've had conversations with angels, what were they like?

If not, what do you envision angels talking about?

Often, people think that an angel can only have conversations about faith issues, or that they only speak when situations are dire. It's my feeling that conversations with angels vary as much as conversations with other people. I'm always curious about the experiences that other people have with angels. If you have spoken with angels, your experience may well be different from mine.

In my case, I had a great variety of conversations with my guardian angel. Some talks were short and some were long; some were emotional, some mundane. Sometimes he just gave me quick warnings, and sometimes we had intense discussions. As far as topics go, my guardian angel would pretty much talk about anything.

For example, one day when my mother had a few friends over at our house, my angel said: *Tell your mother and her friends to buy gold.*

I was just a little boy at the time. When I told them what he said, I'm sure you can imagine their reaction.

They laughed and shook their heads, then looked at my mom and said, "He's got such an active imagination."

She smiled, "Yes, yes he does."

I told them again, "No really, he says you should buy gold."

Naturally, they dismissed me.

Can you guess what happened next?

Just weeks after I shared this information, gold prices skyrocketed. After that, my mother's friends became very interested in my little angel stories. Once, they told me to ask my angel for other ideas.

I asked and his reply was: *Tell them they had their chance, and they should have believed you when you told them the first time.*

After the gold incident, my mother also started to believe my angel stories, but she didn't fully appreciate him until a particular incident occurred.

We lived in a place that had more than its share of shady characters. When my sister was around, I was relatively safe—she was street smart and watchful—but on my own, I was vulnerable. I think I was a pretty typical young kid. I was not particularly observant, and I was relatively trusting by nature. I'm sure I gave my angel numerous opportunities to save me from danger.

We lived across an alley from a white church. One day, when I was walking by the church, a man lurking in the shadows on the side of the building called out to me.

I looked around, spotted him, and replied, "What?"

He motioned for me to come toward him and I obeyed, walking into the alleyway next to him.

He said, "I'll give you twenty dollars if you rub my leg."

I was puzzled and asked, "Twenty dollars, just to rub your leg?"

"Yes."

Twenty dollars in the early seventies was a lot of money and it was a fortune to a poor kid. I thought about it briefly and made a decision.

"Okay," I said.

At this moment, I could hear my angel shouting: *KEITH! What are you doing?*

The man proceeded to pull down his fly and take out his penis. My heart started to pound. I knew I had made a big mistake and there was no one in sight to help me.

I began backing up to move out of the shadows and said, "You know, I may be just a kid, but I definitely know the difference between a leg and a penis, and I'm not rubbing that thing!"

My guardian angel said: *Yell, "MOM!" as loud as you can!*

I did as he said, although my mother was not within earshot. Fearing the arrival of another adult, the man quickly zipped up and fled.

Not only did my angel save me that day, but he also knew that I was confused by what had happened and that I needed further support and direction. As I walked toward home, he explained how some men got a thrill by doing things like that to kids. He encouraged me to go home right away, and tell my mother what had happened.

I followed his instructions. I told my mother the whole story, including the way my angel had intervened. My mother was horrified.

After listening to the story, I remember that she looked up and said to the angel, "Thank you for protecting my Son-shine."

A few weeks later, my mother and I were walking through the park, and I saw the man who had propositioned me. I pointed him out to my mom.

Her expression hardened, and she said, "Stay right here."

She crept up to the man and tapped him on the shoulder. When he turned around, she hit him square in the face, and he went down. I'd never seen her hit anyone in my life.

Who knew she packed such a mean punch?

When he was on the ground, she leaned over him and exclaimed, "If I ever see you within a hundred feet of my child again, I will kill you."

I saw him only one other time. I recognized him walking toward me from a distance. As soon as he saw me, he came off the sidewalk and walked out of his way—*far* out of his way—to avoid getting anywhere near me. Clearly, he remembered my mother's warning!

My mother wasn't always able to defend me but in this case, along with my angel, she had been my protector, and I was grateful.

There were many other occasions when my angel kept me out of harm's way. I learned to do what he said and to do so without questioning. I trusted him completely. He was an angel, after all! I assumed that he knew things I didn't and that he was there to watch over me.

He protected and advised me in innumerable ways. Sometimes he'd tell me to take a different way home, or would warn me not go up an alley or in between houses.

When I was with my friends, and we were planning to do something stupid, I would hear him say, "Tell them you won't do it."

If you think back on your childhood, you'll probably remember how hard it was to say *no* to a group of peers. But I knew and trusted my angel's voice. He gave me the strength to speak up, and in doing so, he kept me out of trouble. I have no doubt that he kept me safe, and out of police custody, many times.

My friends probably benefitted heavily from my guardian angel as well. Often, after I told my friends I wouldn't go along with them, they would drop the plan they had and do something else instead. Kids shift gears easily, so it usually wasn't a big deal. As a result, while he was saving me, it's likely that my guardian angel also saved my friends a great deal of trouble!

A Glimpse Into the Future

Besides giving me advice on what was happening in the present, my guardian angel occasionally gave me clues about the future. One particular conversation gave me a look into my distant future. He gave me precious information that I would keep close to my heart for decades.

A few years after my stepfather's death, my mom finally began getting out of bed on a regular basis. Soon after that, she had a new boyfriend who owned a liquor store a mile or two from our house. We would walk there to visit him. I thoroughly enjoyed these walks with Mom. After living through her grief and depression for those many months, it was wonderful just to walk and talk with her. As a bonus, I'd often get to pick a little toy or some goodies to take home.

On one of these walks, we passed a little girl in front of an apartment complex. I noticed her and thought she was super-cute.

I heard my angel say: *Ah, so you noticed her, did you?*

I said, "Yeah!"

My mom said, "Who are you talking to?"

"My angel."

"Oh, okay."

We continued to walk and as we passed the girl, my heart raced. I looked back once we had cleared the apartment complex. She hadn't noticed me.

My mother and I continued to walk and a few blocks later, my angel said: *That girl will be your wife when you grow up.*

I said, "What?" *Did I hear him right?*

He repeated: *That girl will be your wife when you grow up.*

I said excitedly to Mom, "Turn around. You see that girl? My angel says that she's going to be my wife when I grow up."

Mom replied, "That's nice, Honey."

I know she didn't take it seriously—understandably—but I did. I didn't know how it would happen, but I was sure the angel was right. That little girl, who I had not yet met, would be my wife.

However, I did wonder: *Why was he telling me now—and in such specific detail?*

Was it important that I knew?

Did it matter in a way I didn't realize?

There didn't seem to be a purpose to it. It didn't change anything. He didn't advise me to approach her at the time, and I never felt compelled to.

Still, every time we passed her after that, I not only noticed her but also took note of what she was doing. I checked to see if she looked happy; I always felt good if she did. Sometimes I couldn't see her, but I could hear her playing inside. One time, while my mother and I walked up the alley by her complex, I heard her singing from one of the windows.

Every time we passed her, I would say, "There's my wife."

My mom thought it was cute. Soon, we moved away from that neighborhood and I wondered when—not if, because I believed my angel—I would meet her again.

2

School Years Bullies, Mr. Whitmore, and More Life Lessons

After I finished elementary school, we moved. I don't know how my mother managed it, but we went from living in a shack in the 'hood to living in a two-bedroom duplex in a nice part of Long Beach called Belmont Shore. The house was only four long blocks from the beach.

For me, it was as if we'd won the lottery! I never did ask my mom how she pulled it off; I think part of me didn't really wanted to know. I always knew *why* she did it. She wanted to get Tina and me out of the 'hood.

We were getting older, and she was worried about what would happen to us if we stayed there. Teenagers in the 'hood usually ended up on drugs, in a gang, or in jail—or all three. I know she didn't want that for her kids, and she was willing to make some sacrifices to make sure it didn't happen.

Mom registered me at Will Rogers Junior High for grades seven through nine. My sister had already quit school by that time. Tina dropped out when she was sixteen. She was constantly getting in trouble in high school, and the system wasn't designed for the way she learned. When Mom realized how painful it was for her to be at school, they agreed it was best if she didn't continue.

I felt great about our move. After so many rough years, it seemed like things were finally turning around for us. We now had a nice home in a good neighborhood, and I was looking forward to making friends and attending a new school.

I was ready for this new chapter in my life, and I was sure it was going to be fantastic.

I was wrong.

The Joys of Junior High

Being a poor kid in a good school was not a comfortable situation, and it didn't take me long to realize it. We didn't have money to spend on fashion; much of my clothing was second-hand and probably looked it. My sneakers were old and, of course, they weren't one of the expensive brands that were popular with the kids.

It was a culture shock. All the things the rich kids loved and talked about were new to me. I felt lost in this new world and it didn't take them long to figure out I was an outsider trying to penetrate their elite bubble.

Ah, junior high.

You remember junior high, right?

That wonderful time of life when kids organize themselves into a rigid social structure that is characterized by intolerance and cruelty?

In my school, there were the usual groups: jocks, nerds, stoners, and the cool kids. There was no mixing between groups—not that it mattered to me because I belonged to none of these groups. I suppose I was in the want-to-be group.

What did I want to be?

Like any other teenager, I just wanted to be accepted. But that wasn't to be the case.

I had regular run-ins with both students and teachers, and I was bullied constantly. Even though the location was better than where I had been before, this school was utter torture for me.

The first time I was bullied, I came home and told my mother. She told me to turn the other cheek—a classic motherly response to a young teen. The next day, the student did the same thing to me. I told her again. This time she told me to go and kick his ass—a less classic motherly response!

I asked, "What about turning the other cheek, Mom?"

She said, "Yeah, you do that once. If they mess with you again, kick their ass."

As far as I was concerned I had permission to fight back, so the next time the student messed with me, I took a swing. I ended up in the office with Mr. Whitmore, the vice principal. I told him the truth, including what my mother had said.

I could tell he was amused by my mother's advice: *Turn the other cheek—then kick ass.*

I imagine he had probably never heard such advice from a mother before. He tried not to show his amusement, and I appreciated that. He was unexpectedly kind and funny, while being clear about the rules.

He told me, "We don't discuss religion in school, son, but if I had to take a guess I'd say Jesus probably meant to turn the cheek more than once before clobbering someone."

Unfortunately, it wasn't long before someone else bullied me. Junior high, for me, was a never-ending string of encounters with bullies.

The bane of my existence was a guy named Kirk. I will never forget his name or his face. He messed with me every day. He stalked me in the halls, spat on me, and called me names. He hit me in the back of the head, pulled up my underwear, and repeatedly flicked my ear with his cocked finger. In short, he did whatever he could to embarrass me in front of other students.

One day, Kirk started in on me at recess on the basketball court, and I lost it. I had reached my limit, and I simply went crazy in front of everyone. The basketball court area was full of kids, and the adjacent lunch area was crowded as well, so there were many witnesses.

I screamed I was going to kill him and charged at him full-speed. He turned around and took off running. I chased him off the court and into one of the buildings. He was a faster runner than I was, so he lost me eventually, but from that time on, I had a new reputation—for being crazy.

I actually didn't mind this reputation, because once the other kids thought I was crazy, they left me alone. The incessant bullying had been so terrible that it was a relief just to go to school in peace.

It wasn't long before word got back to Mr. Whitmore, and he called me in to chat. He wasn't calling me in to reprimand me; he wanted to check in with me and make sure I was all right. I loved that about him. He was a good man.

My crazy reputation only worked for a few weeks, after which the bullies started back in on me. If you have any experience with bullies, you know that they come in all types and sizes. The bullies that came after me in school were from different groups. If it wasn't the tough kids, it was the jocks. If it wasn't the jocks, it was the cool kids. They all loved to make my life a living hell. I guess there was a part of me that accepted it, and invited it.

I invited it?

Yes, it's taken me a long time to understand this, but I have come to believe that you either create, promote, or allow everything that happens in your life. But, please—don't misunderstand me—this doesn't excuse the bullies, and it doesn't mean that people who are abused deserve the abuse. It just means that we all have some level of responsibility for what happens in our lives, and we have the ability to change.

In my case, I'm sure I invited this bullying situation for some reason, but of course, at this point in my life, I didn't understand this. I hated every bully-filled moment.

When people are bullied relentlessly, they often will take any opportunity to become bullies themselves. This creates a sad, never-ending cycle of people mistreating people. I would like to say that I never became part of this cycle, but I am sorry to tell you that I, too, became a bully.

I had a wood shop teacher at the junior high who spoke and acted oddly, which made him a target for bullies. Students in his classes often made fun of him, and I'm embarrassed to say I was one of them.

One day, I was harassing him during class, and he got angry. He came over and told me to stand up. He was a tall man, and he towered over me.

He grabbed my arm—hard—and growled angrily, "I'm tired of the shit I'm getting from you!"

He continued to yell at me while squeezing the life out of my arm and digging his fingernails into my flesh. I told him he was hurting me. I told him repeatedly to let go of me. He didn't listen and continued his tirade. I asked him one more time to let me go. Again, there was no response.

I balled up my fist and hit him.

He let me go, looked at me in shock, then said, "You go to Mr. Whitmore and tell him that you're such a big man that you hit your teacher."

At Mr. Whitmore's office, I looked him in the eye, sighed, and told him the whole truth; both what the teacher had said and done, and what I had said and done. He asked me to show him my arm, which had fresh, red fingernail marks where the teacher had broken the skin on the tender underside of my arm. It was proof that everything I had said was true.

Mr. Whitmore called the teacher to the office, asked me to leave, and took the teacher to task. I could hear them from the outer waiting room. I heard Mr. Whitmore tell the teacher to apologize to me. Mr. Whitmore said if I decided not to accept the teacher's apology, I could press charges, and he would lose his job. The teacher came out and found me, and sincerely apologized.

When you have experience with bullying *and* being bullied, as I did, you get to understand both sides well. I knew I had harassed that teacher; I had played the bully's role in this interaction. I was, therefore, partially responsible for what had happened. I accepted his apology. I was beginning to understand how easy it was to take personal frustrations out on someone who didn't deserve it. It was an important lesson for me.

Because of all my challenges in junior high, by the time I graduated, Mr. Whitmore and I were on a first name basis. Fortunately for me, we eventually became good friends. On a ninth grade field trip to a Navy shipyard, Mr. Whitmore joined us. When I got on the bus, he was sitting by himself, and I went right for the seat next to him. He was surprised, but, truly, there was no place else I wanted to be. He and I had great conversations on the way to the ship, during our lunch break, and all the way home.

Mr. Whitmore had met with my mother a few times and had seen that she wasn't a strong role model. I don't know if he was aware of the extent of her emotional disability, but he knew she was inconsistent in her parenting, and that she gave out inappropriate advice for most situations—often promoting violence. He also knew I had no father around to help, and I think he felt a bit sorry for me.

However, it was clear to me, even then, that pity wasn't the only reason he treated me the way he did. I could see that he truly cared; he was dedicated to helping all his students. The way I saw him handle and respond to us set an important example for me. Instead of being harsh, treating me like a loser, or abusing his position of power, he would always take time to talk with me. He gave me solid reasons for making other choices—choices that didn't include violence.

Even when he had to suspend me—and he did on many occasions—he'd explain exactly why he was suspending me, and in addition, he would present me with some strategies I could use to handle similar situation in the future. He knew the strategies he suggested might not always work—and I might not always choose them—but he was he was trying to stock me up with alternatives to the behavior that was getting me in trouble.

As you have already read, I hadn't learned many effective tactics for conflict resolution in my childhood. Mr. Whitmore's advice was sorely needed. He demonstrated firm, but compassionate, leadership, and I had never experienced that before. I felt closer to him than any adult I had encountered at that school, or any other.

When I look back on my adolescence, I see Mr. Whitmore as a critical protective force in my life—rather like an angel. If he hadn't stepped in from time to time, I know I would have ended up in big trouble in school. I will always be grateful to him for his thoughtful guidance.

Fortunately, when I wasn't in school, I was having a great time in our Belmont Shore neighborhood. I had some friends, and I spent my after-school hours playing on the street and the beach.

I was creative and smart as an adolescent, which sometimes got me in trouble, but also allowed me access to some interesting opportunities. I remember one in particular. When I was twelve, and Christmas was approaching, I wanted to be able to buy my mom and sister some real gifts for the holiday, but I didn't have any money. I came up with a plan.

I had seen that there were inexpensive Christmas cards—just ninety-nine cents a box—at a store called Pick 'n' Save. At that low price, I thought I could make a profit if I bought some and then resold them at a higher price. I didn't have any money, so I had to ask my mother for a five-dollar loan. She asked me why, and I shared my plan with her. She liked the idea, and she funded my first entrepreneurial adventure.

I bought five boxes of cards, and then I went home and changed into some clothes that were wrinkly and dirty. I went door to door selling those cards in our well-to-do neighborhood. I told my customers my story—that I was trying to make money to buy Christmas presents for my mother and sister. I sold bigger boxes of cards for seven dollars, and smaller boxes for five.

I sold out of cards in about an hour. One sweet lady loved my cause so much that she gave me the seven dollars and told me to keep the cards. When I counted up, I found I had earned thirty-eight dollars—in only an hour. My eyes grew wide and my mind started plotting my next move.

I went home, got my skateboard, skated back to the Pick 'n Save, and bought twenty boxes of cards with my earnings. I continued to go door-to-door selling the cards in the neighborhood until I had earned about three hundred fifty dollars!

What do you think of that wheeler-dealer?

When I think back on him, I can't help smiling at that smart and funny kid.

I went Christmas shopping for my mother and sister with my earnings. I was also able to get something for my grandmother, so all three of the awesome women in my life got a great gift that year. I don't remember all the gifts, but I do remember picking out an elegant fourteen-karat gold necklace for my mother.

This wasn't the only time my mother supported me in exploring my own ideas. I so appreciate her for that. Although there were many parenting tasks she didn't do well, as you have read, she helped me to learn self-reliance, and she taught me not to be afraid to put my ideas into action. In doing so, my mother gave me the freedom to explore some of the most important aspects of life.

My mother also had an uncanny knack for predicting events that were going to happen to me and to my sister. I wonder now if she had her own angels speaking to her.

Have you ever had a feeling that tells you *something* is about to happen?

Have you ever felt a strong sense of danger about setting off on a particular path?

Whenever you have one of these feelings, it is likely an angel is talking to you, and is trying to help you choose a safe and happy path. My mother never gave me the idea that she listened to angels, but she did pay attention to those feelings when she had them. Of course, I didn't often recognize the value of what she said to me. Like most kids, I rarely heeded my mother's warnings.

For example, one day, when I was going to go skateboarding, Mom stopped me at the door.

She said, "Please, don't go skating today. You'll break your wrist."

I replied, "No, I won't!"

When she persisted, I rolled my eyes, and told her to leave me alone.

I stormed out and started skating around the neighborhood. Within a few hours, I had fallen and—you guessed it—my wrist was badly hurt. She took me to the emergency room. I had a hairline fracture. Big surprise.

Looking at her with amazement, I remember asking her that day, "Did you see it, or did you create it?"

I should have listened to my mother's premonitions. Perhaps my mother's angels were trying to look out for Tina and me. My own guardian angel was always there for me, but during this time, my mind was preoccupied with the angst of adolescence, and I think that sometimes made it harder to hear him. From time to time, however, he stepped in when I needed him most.

An Angel Saves My Life for the Third Time

I was a boy scout for a few years during this period. In the summer, scouts of different ages went to camp together. I tagged along with the older boys every moment I could. I'm sure I was a regular pest.

One day at camp, the older boys walked down a trail, and I followed. When I got there, they were all hanging out on the edge of a cliff. The rocks were slippery, coated with sandy soil, but they were enjoying the danger. Flirting with disaster, they were sitting way out on the edge.

You can imagine the way I felt, watching them. To me, it looked like the most fun anyone could ever have. I simply *had* to get out there.

I begged to join them and kept on begging when they said no. They did their best to shoo me away, but I was a stubborn kid, and I persisted. Finally, they got tired of my whining and agreed to let me come out on the cliff.

For all my pleading, I was scared, but I didn't let on.

As long as I don't look down, I'll be fine, I told myself.

I got myself out to where the other boys were, and I was fine for a while, but when we got up to leave, I slipped. I fell onto my belly and started sliding down the slippery slope. The next thing I knew, my body went over the edge of the cliff, and I slipped out into empty space.

Just as I was sure I was a goner, a hand reached out and grabbed my wrist. I was hanging by one hand, my feet were kicking, and I was screaming at the top of my lungs.

To pull me up, they formed a human chain, and somehow, by the grace of God, got me back up to safety. It sounds like something straight out of action-adventure movie, but it really happened.

The older boys lectured me all the way back to camp, and I was sworn to secrecy. They knew they would be in trouble for going out on the cliff in the first place.

I am certain that my guardian angel helped me that day.

How else could that boy have held me on that slippery slope?

I wasn't a big kid, but I wasn't that small either. He shouldn't have been able to hold me by the wrist, with my full body weight hanging in space. There is no way he would have been able to do it—without help. This was the third time an angel saved my life.

Football, Horses, and Goodbye to Junior High

Time marched on, and finally, I graduated from junior high and could look ahead to a new school—the high school. I was hopeful that things would change for me once I was in high school, but like most kids, I lived in the moment—and at that moment, I was glad just to have junior high behind me. A long summer stretched out ahead of me.

Looking back now, I would say that junior high was one of the worst periods of my childhood. There is nothing in it that I would ever want to repeat, or even revisit. However, I have to say that there were a few elements—just a few—that were positive.

It's always good to recognize positives and possibilities, so let me list them for you. You've already read about Mr. Whitmore. He became a wonderful father figure for me, and I am forever grateful for his help. I had a fantastic art teacher in seventh grade. I learned to type—which is a skill serving me at this very moment. I had a girlfriend at the end of ninth grade, and I had developed some good friendships as well.

During the summer after junior high, my mother dated a black man named John. He was cool—a great guy—and I felt relaxed and comfortable around him. I should say that I've always felt more comfortable around black people than white people, so much so that, at times, I have felt certain that I was dropped into the wrong body at birth!

John was the coach of an all-black football team across town in Long Beach. I had always wanted to play football, and if I was going to play, it surely wasn't going to be with all the white kids in Belmont Shore, who weren't exactly known for winning. If I was going to play, I wanted to win.

I asked if I could try out for John's team. My mother was opposed, but John convinced her that trying out would be character building for me, and she shouldn't worry, because my chances of actually making the team were slim to none. After hearing that, she agreed.

I was not exactly met with open arms at the tryouts. If I had ever experienced true racial profiling as a white kid, this was it. They did not appreciate me being there. They were not feeling it. Just having me try out was offensive to them—to their very core. The adults clearly felt the same as the kids.

In fact, the other coach pulled John aside and asked him, "Why the hell did you bring him here?"

John replied, "He's my girlfriend's kid. He's a good kid—just give him a shot."

The other coach reluctantly agreed.

We started out by warming up. They put us into rows, and we did stretches. After stretching, we ran the bleachers. When they had us good and winded, they divided us into groups by the position we intended to play.

I wasn't sure what position I should play, so they assigned me to a group. They put me with the linemen. I looked around me and saw that all the guys in this group were extra big—way taller and way bigger than me.

I didn't say anything, but I wondered: *Why did they put me in this group?*

We ran drills as the coaches watched and took notes.

All day long, I was taking verbal shots from the guys:

"Go home, white boy. Why are you here anyway?"

"What are you trying to prove? You ain't gonna make it on this team."

"Why don't you just go play with some white-boy team?"

At first, I wondered: *Why were these guys so down on me, when they didn't even know me?*

I hadn't expected this reaction, which might seem naïve to you. At the time, however, I was only thinking about wanting to play football for a good team. As I said before, I was more comfortable with black people than white, so I wasn't thinking about our racial differences as a problem.

Hearing all the put-downs at the tryouts made me think about it from their point of view. The more I thought about it, the more I understood why they were treating me this way. To them, I was just this white boy, who lived on the other side of town, trying to get on their team.

However, just because I understood why they didn't want me there didn't mean I was going to quit. I had never quit anything in my life and wasn't about to start that day.

Much of the day was a blur, but I'll never forget one part. The coaches put us into two lines. They chose one person, then another, and put them side by side. Then they chose another two people and put them side by side behind the first pair.

When they got to me, they chose the biggest guy there, and put him next to me. This guy was at least six feet tall and must have weighed 230–250 pounds. He was an absolute giant. I was five foot five at best and probably weighed in at 160–170 pounds.

You probably know what was about to happen, but I didn't at the time.

When we were all lined up, they proceeded to take one person from each side, had them face each other and get into a three-point football stance—crouched down with one hand on the ground. They would blow the whistle, and the two guys would try to tackle each other to the ground.

After watching from down the line, I took another peek at my partner. He looked bigger than ever. My pairing seemed dreadfully out of balance. I could see that most of the other guys were evenly matched to each other in size and weight.

I was going to have to try and tackle—or perhaps be killed by—this giant.

The closer we got to the front of the line, the faster my heart pounded. They moved quickly and, before I knew it, it was our turn. I assumed the position. Time felt like it was moving in slow motion. The guy across from me was looking at me like he was going to kill me. The whistle blew, and everything shifted into real time. We launched toward each other, and he ran me right over, much like a bulldozer rips up hot pavement in the summer.

I could hear the watching crowd let out a cry as I was leveled. Everyone around me grinned as I gathered myself up off the ground and walked to the back of the line.

The line slowly moved forward again. My heart began to race as I got caught up in the fear again. We reached the front of the line, assumed the position, the whistle blew, and again, I was leveled. It took a little longer this time to get up, but I did, and proceeded to the back of the line.

The big guy looked at me as if to say: *Would you just quit?*

I shook my head and stared at the ground. If I kept the same strategy, I was just going to get flattened again. It was time to make a different plan.

I thought to myself: *I'm not going down this time. I took judo; I know that if you hit a guy low, he'll topple. He's like twice my size; it should be easy to hit him low. He's cocky now. He thinks I'm a pushover so he'll lighten up. I can do this. I can take him.*

We had reached the front of the line again.

The coach sighed, "Are you sure you want to go again?"

I straightened up and gave a resounding, "Yes, sir!"

We assumed the position, and the whistle blew. I launched forward with everything I had, staying extremely low to the ground, and aiming for his lower legs. I wrapped my arms around his knees and bulldozed forward with all my might.

The giant toppled over, and I landed on top of him.

As I lay there, looking straight into his eyes, he said, "Good job, Boy."

This time, the sounds from the crowd were different—instead of mocking laughter, there were sounds of puzzlement: *What the…?*

As we stood up, the giant man looked at me again, and in front of everybody, he said, chuckling, "You're all right!"

That shifted everything. I had actually earned the respect of, not only the giant man, but of the coaches and the other players.

Most important—I made the team.

We made it all the way to the finals that year. In the championship game, we got pummeled by the other team. The players on the opposing team were some of the oldest-looking teenagers I had ever seen. Obviously, they had fudged a few records and birth certificates because we were lining up against grown-ass men. It was a beat down, but we learned a lot in the process.

I enjoyed playing football and other sports with John. We did some other fun activities together as well. I respected John and I liked his company.

I never talked to John about my angels, but I once had a profound angel day with him at a racetrack. John had a son of his own, and one day he invited both of us to the track. He gave us twenty dollars each, and he said he would place our bets for us. He told us that, whatever we won, we could keep. I didn't know the first thing about horse racing so I asked him to tell me how it worked. He explained the odds system, and he told me how he picked horses.

As we looked at the first round of horses walking the track, I heard my angel whispering in my ear.

He said: *Look at the horses. How are they feeling right now? Which one looks confused? Which one looks angry? Which one looks relaxed and happy?*

As he asked all these questions, I answered by pointing to different horses.

When I pointed to the horse that looked relaxed and happy, he said: *Choose that one.*

I told John, and even though the odds were five-to-one, he placed the bet for me. My horse won the race.

John celebrated the victory, but called it *beginner's luck.* My angel, again, helped me select horses to bet on in the next race. While John and his son looked at odds and written information, I looked at the horses. My next winner won at ten-to-one odds.

After picking the winner three races in a row, John asked me which horse was going to win the next race and then, he placed my bet and put his bet on my choice as well. I won all but one race that day. I forget how much money I left the track with, but I remember that my mother was not too happy about where it came from. She tried to make me give the money back, but John wouldn't take it. He did let me pay him back the initial twenty dollars, but made me keep the rest.

High School, Truancy, and New Expectations

As the summer waned and high school approached, I did some soul searching. I was dreading the start of school, but was hopeful that high school would be better than junior high. I contemplated my options.

What could I do to make sure that the next three years were not like the last three?

There were no easy answers. My goal was to make friends, have fun—and not be bullied.

But how could I make sure no one bullied me in high school?

I began to formulate a plan. I knew who the bullies were in the junior high, and I knew which ones were coming with me to the high school. I may or may not have been on their targeting radar, but I wasn't going to chance it. I decided to make certain they didn't continue bullying me.

So, during the first few days of school, one by one, I tracked down these junior high bullies. I approached each one from behind, tapped him on the shoulder, and when he turned around, I grabbed him by the shirt and threw him up against the locker or wall—or whatever was nearby.

I pushed my face right up to each one and threatened, "I may have been a doormat in junior high, but don't mess with me in high school, or you'll be sorry!"

Obviously, I was still relying on primitive methods of conflict resolution.

At the time, it seemed to work. I did have a few altercations in high school, but not nearly as many as in the years before. In truth, I don't know if it was my threats that made the difference. These kids were starting from scratch themselves and had their own concerns about fitting in. In retrospect, it is possible that they wouldn't have gone after me in this new environment—but I wasn't taking any chances.

The only part of junior high I was sad to leave behind was Mr. Whitmore. However, there was a pleasant surprise waiting for me on my first day at the high school.

While I was in line to get my lunch, I looked into the cafeteria, and guess who I saw?

It was Mr. Whitmore, leaning against the wall, hands by his sides in his usual posture.

I went over to greet him and exclaimed, "Mr. Whitmore! What are you doing here?"

He told me that, during the summer, he had been offered a position at the high school, and he had taken the job.

He smiled, "You didn't think you could get rid of me that easily, did you?"

I was never so glad to see an adult in my life. I took it as a good sign—an omen that high school would be a good experience for me. However, even with Mr. Whitmore around, my poor behavior continued through high school. One of my big issues was truancy.

In high school, the first time I stayed home sick, my mother wrote a note excusing my absence. I needed to take the note to school the next day because a note from a parent was required after every absence. I took the note my mother had written for me, threw it away, and wrote my own. I already had mastered my mother's signature in junior high, so that was no problem.

You may be wondering why I swapped my mother's note with my mine. If you're asking, you don't have the criminal mind that I had as a teenager.

I'll explain. You see, I planned to cut school with some regularity in the future, and I wanted the office to have only *my* handwriting on file. So, I replaced her note with mine.

Are you impressed? Kind of an ingenious plan, wasn't it?

It worked well initially; my letter went into the file and from that point on, I took days off as I wanted and wrote my own notes when I was ready to return to school.

Of course, although I was smart enough to come up with that sneaky plan, I wasn't at all sensible with my cutting schedule. One semester, I ditched thirty-two days, so the truancy board was notified. The truant officers showed up at our doorstep and told my mother how many days I had missed.

Where was I at that moment?

I was hiding, of course. I was hiding in my room, just like any kid in potentially big trouble. From there, I could hear every word.

My mother told the officers, "Yes, I know he missed thirty-two days, and he was sick every one of those days. You can go now."

I'm sure they didn't believe her, but they left the porch, and drove off in their car. I was saved.

Then, Mom came into my room. She did not look happy. I started to speak, but then thought the better of it, because of the look on her face. She proceeded to unload on me the type of wrath that, until that day, I had only seen directed toward my sister.

Lesson learned.

Wow, she was mad. I know now that she was angry that I had deceived her, but in addition, her attitude toward my education had changed, and I hadn't expected that. I think she was starting to get worried that I was going to end up a high school dropout. Perhaps she was thinking she wanted at least one of her kids to graduate from high school.

At this stage of life, there are so many changes to adapt to, and my mother's attitude was one of them. Teen maturity grows in fits and starts, and it comes with changes in perspective—on your own life and on what's happening around you. Expectations change as well. You probably had similar experiences as a teenager.

My mother's standards and expectations had changed—and mine would change, too, as time passed.

I was poor as a teenager, and for poor teenagers, the future doesn't offer much. However, I had big dreams, and I had been raised to look at the possibilities of life—not to dwell on the negative. In the short-term, I did want to finish high school, but I wasn't worried about that, not at the moment anyway. I was focused on my long-term dreams, which were about fame and fortune.

As a teenager, money issues impacted me differently than they did when I was a child. Now, I went to school with wealthy classmates. Every day, I could see the difference that money—or the lack of it—made in our teenage lives. Without having to work after school and on weekends, my classmates had money for fashionable clothing and teenage toys, for concerts and for dates with girls. They could afford to plan for expensive colleges.

I, however, had to work in order to have any money at all. Remember, we were on welfare and living in a well-to-do neighborhood, so my mother didn't exactly have any extra money she could hand me. She was always just scraping by, budgeting, doing whatever she could to make sure we could stay in that good neighborhood, where she hoped she could keep me from gangs, drugs, and prison.

I remember saving up so I would have enough money to go to the prom. To make it extra special, my friend, David, and I arranged to have dinner with our dates at a fancy restaurant. We went to the restaurant ahead of time and pre-paid for our meal. David's family knew the owners, so they gave us a great deal, and from the time we arrived, we were given first-class treatment all the way. When it came time to pay, all we had to do was sign our names on the ticket. No money was exchanged; only our signatures were given. Our girls looked at each other and raised their eyebrows, as if they were impressed.

How great that felt! I wanted to feel that way all the time.

I had a friend in high school named Russ. He had a younger brother and a great dad—Russell Sr. When I had dinner with their family one night, his father asked me lots of questions. He asked me about *real* things—he wondered how I felt about life and current events. He treated me like an adult, and I liked that.

Russell was interested in me. He loved my sense of humor and my music. For me, that kind of attention from an adult was a rare and precious thing. It is probably evident to you that I was especially hungry for attention and guidance from father figures.

One time, Russell invited me to come to a big dinner party. At the party were several business owners who owned different types of companies. These were smart, educated, and successful people, and they treated me with interest and respect.

I remember Russell asking me that night, "What do want to be when you grow up?"

I told him my plan. I was going to be a rock star in my twenties and thirties, a best-selling author and speaker in my forties, and a famous film director from my fifties on. Of course, I was also going to have an incredibly beautiful wife by my side. We would have a big, five-bedroom house in the mountains.

Quite a plan, right?

I told you I had dreams!

Russell said something in response that has stuck in my mind to this day: "Keith, if you find a job doing something that you love, you will never work a day in your life."

I took out my guitar, and I played and sang for the group. They were gracious and appreciative. That was one hell of an experience for me. For me, it was if the party had been held in my honor for the sole purpose of being able to rub elbows with successful business people.

In retrospect, I can see that these social encounters helped to make me comfortable around people with money. Although I didn't know it at the time, having these experiences early in life would benefit me later. Socially, a poor kid like me would likely have been uncomfortable with wealthy people—so many who grow up in poverty are resentful of those with monetary success. But because I had some mentors like Russell, I didn't grow up feeling that way at all.

My life in high school was much better than in junior high. My grades weren't too good, a fact that would come to haunt me later, but I wasn't bullied much, and I had some good friends—and good times. I was somewhat of a reckless teenager, like many, and I didn't have a disciplined home life to keep me in check.

My recklessness almost cost me my life when I was seventeen.

No Brakes: An Angel Saves My Life Once Again

My best friend, Timar, bought a 1969 Ford Mustang for his first car. We spent a few months tooling around and having fun in the car. We lived close to a long strip of straight roadway. It ran next to a water skiing arena and had only one stop sign along a stretch of two miles. One night, hardly anyone was on the street, so Timar decided to open it up to see just how fast we could go.

The car reached ninety miles an hour, and Timar decided to blow past the stop sign. We continued along the straightaway, and we were approaching one hundred miles an hour, when we saw a red light and cars up ahead. Timar put his foot on the brake.

The car kept going just as fast. We were not slowing down.

Timar pumped the brakes—and pumped them again.

He looked over at me and said, "Dude, *no brakes!*"

He continued to pump and pump and, eventually, the brakes locked up. We skidded toward an intersection where a line of cars was waiting for the light to turn green. He came up to the cars in front of us, swung the car to the left, and then, pulled the steering wheel back to the right. We slammed into a cement island, and the car hit the power box that ran the light at that intersection. I saw glass break, and heard metal crunch, as my neck snapped right and then left. Things went dark for a second, and then—

> *—my life flashed before my eyes. I didn't see every moment in the flash, but I saw all the main events that had had a major impact on my life up until that point. My birth, me as a toddler, birthday parties, my mother crying and me supporting her with my love, the cliff incident in Utah, the scout camp scare, my trips to the ER with ear infections, and other major important learning events.*
>
> *All of a sudden, I saw another white flash and then images started to go in reverse taking me back to the beginning. When I got past childbirth, I saw another white flash and—*

—I snapped back in the present moment. We found ourselves sitting in the car on the side of the road, just to the right of intersection.

"My dad is going to kill me," I heard Timar say.

It sounded like his voice was coming from far away. As I sat there, my surroundings gradually came into focus. I could see the interior of the car, and I could hear the engine running. The car was idling, and it was purring like a kitten. I couldn't see any damage to the windshield. In my field of view, I couldn't see any damage at all.

"Are you okay?" I asked Timar.

He said he was.

I asked him, "Did you hear glass breaking?"

He said that he did.

"Did your life flash before your eyes?" I asked.

"Yes," he said.

We decided to get out, look at the car, and see how bad the damage was. When I came around the car, Timar was standing there, looking at the side of the car, and shaking his head in disbelief. There was not a scratch or a dent on that car. Only the left rear hubcap was missing. It was sitting in the middle of the intersection.

There was not another car in sight. Timar collected the hubcap and put it back on the car. We looked over to the spot where we had hit the island. There was a jagged slice running up the side of the curb, leading right up to the power box. His tire rim had carved out physical proof that we had not only hit the island, but hit the box as well.

But there was no damage to the car—at all.

We looked at each other, saying nothing, and got back in the car. We just sat there in silence for what seemed like a lifetime.

You've already read about my previous near-death experiences. I knew at this moment that an angel had once again intervened. I had always had a strong belief in a higher power, and I knew this higher power wanted me on the earth for a reason. All my life, I had possessed this strong spiritual connection, but I knew Timar never had. He was still sitting in silence, trying to process what had happened. I decided to break the silence.

I asked Timar again, "So, you heard glass break, right?"

He nodded, "Yeah."

"And you heard metal crunching?"

He nodded again.

I said, "And now we are sitting here in a car with no physical damage, but there is proof over there that it all happened."

Timar looked up to the heavens and took a breath, then looked down at the steering wheel.

He turned his head toward me and said, "And all this time I thought you were full of crap about the God thing."

He spent the next day telling me about how much greener the trees were and just how beautiful everything was on this earth. He was grateful to be alive. As time passed, however, his memory of how it went down faded from his mind.

Have you ever had a miraculous experience like this?

If so, what was your reaction?

It is common for people to feel initially humbled and filled with wonder, but those feelings often fade rapidly. Because this type of experience is beyond what your mind can accept, denial can quickly take over, and erase the truth.

In this case, I guess Timar learned what he needed to learn—I can tell you that it was the last time we flew down that straightaway at a hundred miles an hour.

It was the fourth time an angel had stepped in to save my life, but this experience was different for me than the others. In the past, my angel had intervened to prevent bad things from happening to me. This time, it felt like something catastrophic had happened, but time had been reversed so that the results were erased.

It wouldn't be the last time I would be presented with this kind of experience.

The angel had also saved Timar, and for that, I was so grateful.

I wondered: *What if I hadn't been in the car with him? Would he still be alive? Would he have been saved by his own angel?*

I didn't have an answer to those questions.

Pass or Fail?

After my junior year, my guidance counselor told me that I was at risk of not graduating. I would have to pass *every* class in my last year to qualify. I couldn't believe it; it hadn't occurred to me that it was possible that I might not graduate.

You may ask—didn't I know how bad my grades were?

Well, I guess, like many teenagers, I wasn't paying attention. Grades never seemed important. School never seemed important. I had never even tried to get good grades. Most of the time, my mother didn't care one way or another. She didn't keep track of my grades, and she believed me when I told her that I had tried my best.

It was the truth—well, sort of.

I had tried my best to do the least possible, while partying and having a good time.

I wondered: *Am I a complete idiot? Have I learned anything?*

The most important practical question was: *Could I actually pass every class?*

I did want to graduate. I decided that, for once, I would do the work, and see how I measured up. I knuckled down, paid attention in class, did the homework, and studied.

The first semester of my senior year, I got four A's and two B's. The second half of the year I took Political Science, which was the bane of my existence. Even though I did all the work and participated in class, when it came time to test, I would freeze up and not remember anything. When I took the final, I was quite sure I bombed.

I was passing everything else, but that wouldn't matter. This one failure would keep me from graduating. With dread in my heart, I went in to collect my grade.

I looked my teacher in the eye and asked him, "Did I pass?"

He winked at me and said, "I think you may have just squeaked by."

He had given me a C. I started to tear up.

He said, "Your homework grades and your class participation were exemplary. There is no way I could be responsible for you not graduating when you tried so hard. You earned this grade."

With traditional school finished, I had grown up in many ways. I now knew several important things about life and about myself:

- My mother's choices were not mine, and didn't have to influence mine.
- I could take control of social situations and not let the bullies of the world be a part of my life.
- All around me, there were mentors and people to learn from.
- When I applied myself, I could do better than just get by; I could truly succeed.

And my angel?

He was never far away.

3

College
My Soul Mate, Fresno, Drugs, and a New Friend

After my first year of college, I reconnected with an old friend, Rob. He told me that he was going to go with our high school's current graduating class to Magic Mountain, a local roller coaster chain, but he had a dilemma.

He was attending with his new girlfriend, Tina, *and* with his old girlfriend, Rebecca. It was an awkward situation, and he asked for my help.

Rebecca had won tickets to Magic Mountain while they were dating, and she had promised to take him. She was determined to keep her promise even though they were no longer together. He asked me if I would come along to keep Rebecca occupied.

I had met Rebecca once, briefly. I had never told anyone, but I was certain she was the girl from my childhood, the little girl my guardian angel had told me I would marry. All my life, I had envisioned her and waited for her. When I met her, it was puzzling that she was dating someone else, but I trusted that my angel knew what he was doing.

It may seem strange to you that I didn't seek her out after I recognized her. I knew somehow that it wasn't time for us yet, but I was certain we would meet again. I was confident that she would eventually be my wife.

Now she was single. He invited me to come later that day to meet her. When I got there, I could tell she was uncomfortable with the situation, so I didn't stay long. I would have the whole night at Magic Mountain to get to know her, and I didn't want to be pushy.

We all met at Tina's house before going to Magic Mountain. As we prepared to leave, Rob pulled out a bag of magic mushrooms and divided what he had into four servings. We ate them and headed out. They didn't come on strong until we were inside the amusement park, where there were lots of lights and people.

Things went fine at the amusement park, but Rebecca was a bit withdrawn. We spoke here and there, but mostly she walked by my side and stayed away from Rob and Tina. Clearly, she felt awkward. She wanted to keep the promise she had made, even though it wasn't comfortable for her. I liked that about her.

At one point, I told the group a story about a concert I had recently attended. It was the US Festival, the largest concert since Woodstock. Almost every band I liked at that time had played at the festival. While there, I had met many interesting people, including a lovely woman from Berkley. She was big into punk rock. She was funny, smart, and had great ideas about how the world should be.

When I was telling them about her, I remember saying, "I sure miss that girl. I wish I could see her right now."

As I finished that sentence, I looked about twenty feet in front of me and there she stood—the girl from the concert!

We locked eyes and she screamed out loud, "No way, I was just talking about you to my friends!"

I said, "Holy crap, so was I!"

We took the opportunity to catch up as our friends stared in disbelief, wondering how we had manifested each other like that. Rebecca seemed happy to have me occupied by another girl instead focusing on her.

It was late when we decided we would head out. Rob admitted he was too buzzed to drive all the way home, but he thought he could make it to a hotel. We piled in the car and got onto the freeway. Eventually we found a hotel and took a single room for the four of us.

As we're walking up the stairs to our room, Rebecca turned to me and said, "Just so you know, you're not going to get lucky tonight!"

I smiled. I was fine with that. I had waited eleven years to see her again. I was in no rush.

As soon as we got to the room, Rob and Tina were all over each other. They were kissing and groping, and clothes were flying everywhere. It was as if we weren't in the room. Both Rebecca and I were supremely uncomfortable as they made love wildly—and loudly—in our presence.

It wasn't easy, but we did our best to ignore them and, as we came down from the mushrooms, we finally started to connect. We talked for hours, long after Rob and Tina were asleep. We were still talking when the sun came up.

I learned that she lived with her grandmother. Her mother, like mine, was a mess and hadn't been involved much in her upbringing. Since we were hitting it off, I decided I would be honest and tell her my whole story.

I thought: *If this is the girl I am meant to be with, then she won't freak out.*

I not only told Rebecca about my family, but about my angel. I told her I had seen her many times when she was a young girl, and I recounted what my angel had said about her. She was intrigued. I could tell she wasn't certain the story was actually true. However, I also sensed that she knew I was being honest with her—that I believed what I was saying was true. In the few hours we had known each other, she had come to trust me enough to know that I was telling her my truth.

Eventually, we woke Rob and Tina so we could drive home. When we got close to Long Beach, Rebecca asked Rob if we could take a quick detour. He agreed, so we took the exit to the neighborhood where we had grown up.

Rebecca said, "Okay, Keith, if your story is true, you'll be able to show me where I lived."

I said, "No problem."

I gave Rob directions to the apartment building.

When we pulled up in front of the building, I said, "This is where you used to play with your dolls and toys."

I asked Rob to take a left up the alley that ran next to the side of the apartment building.

When we got to a certain window, I told him to stop and said, "That was your bedroom. Sometimes I could hear you playing in there when my mom and I walked by."

Rebecca's jaw was open, and she was clearly blown away. She had not expected this. I could feel something shift at that moment.

Years later, she told me, "That day, I was thinking there was no way that you could know these things without them being true. And if it was true that the angel told you that we were supposed to be together, the least I could do was give this a chance."

Young Love

Rebecca and I were inseparable after that. We stayed at Tina's apartment for weeks, seeing no one but each other. We swapped stories from our childhood. I shared with her how my father had left and moved to Virginia and about my mother's depression. I shared all my guardian angel stories, and more.

Rebecca shared stories about her alcoholic mother, how her father had left them when she was young, leaving her with her grandmother. We went to the deepest level we could at our age. We shared our fears, our worries, and our core beliefs.

After a few weeks, we realized we needed to check in with our families. Her grandmother and my mother were both furious with us. They thought we were dead. They had everyone looking for us. Rebecca was grounded by her grandmother so we spent some time apart, but the memories of our time together got us through.

Being together was like a fairy tale for both of us. Everything was brand new and exciting. This young love was so special. Imagine going into a relationship knowing you are meant to be with that person. The information I had received from my angel was coming true. Every day was exciting; every moment was incredible. She was adventurous, and so was I. We had so much fun together.

One night, we decided to check out a new residential building, hoping to find one of the empty condominiums with an unlocked door. We walked the halls, trying doorknobs, and finally found a three-bedroom condominium on the top floor that was filled with new appliances and nothing else. We went from room to room, discussing exactly what we would put in each room if we lived there.

In our minds, we furnished this beautiful place. We could see it exactly the way we had imagined it. We went to our master bedroom where we laid down on our king-size bed and made love. Of course, in reality, we made love on the floor. We fell asleep together and didn't get home until early the next morning. For staying out late again, Rebecca was grounded, but it was worth it.

I was crazy nervous the first time I met her grandmother. I was reasonably sure she wouldn't like me.

Why would she?

Everything she knew of me was negative. She knew that Rebecca was with me when she disappeared for two weeks. Then, the night we spent at the condo, Rebecca didn't call to let her know we would be late. Even after Rebecca was no longer grounded, she was constantly arguing with her grandmother and often stayed out late—with me.

Needless to say, our first meeting didn't go well. Rebecca's grandmother made it clear that she didn't like me. I didn't like her either. She was the most negative person I had ever met. Because she didn't like me, she was determined to break us up. Somehow, Rebecca seemed unfazed by her grandmother's intentions.

Eventually, I took Rebecca to meet my mother. The situation there was no better. I was her Son-shine, and my mother didn't want anyone to come between us. But neither my mother nor Rebecca's grandmother could keep us apart, and because of what my angel had told me, I never worried.

Being in love at such a young age creates a world of firsts, and we enjoyed every one. We did everything together, made promises to one another, and dreamed into the future. We promised each other that, if we ever had a child, we would never divorce. We both knew how much it had hurt us as children, and we would not do that to our child.

Being in love at a young age also creates a world of new challenges. I had confidence in our relationship, and I know some of that confidence came from my angel. Rebecca, however, didn't have the same kind of faith in us. After a few months, she became nervous about our relationship and asked for some time apart. She said she needed time to think.

I didn't understand this. To me things were going well. We had a life filled with love and adventure.

What could she need to think about?

A Time of Uncertainty and Doubt

Because I loved her, I agreed. Time passed, and she came back and told me she was ready, and apologized for breaking up with me. We got back together, and all was well.

Or so I thought.

Things didn't feel the same after that. Our relationship was okay, but not as incredible as before. Doubt had entered our relationship and, sadly, it was to be a powerful force between us.

We had both grown up without good role models for long-term relationships. We both had poor communication and conflict resolution skills. She had trouble trusting. Her fear of abandonment, instilled in her by a father who left when she was young, made an impact on us.

Her behavior often confused and hurt me. There were incidences of infidelity—some of them with friends of mine.

If we were so in love, and meant to be together, why did I have to deal with this?

Why would she be unfaithful?

Because of my angel encounter, instead of breaking up or giving up, I chose to forgive and try to work through these issues. I felt like our love was deep enough and worth any amount of work to keep it together.

When I met Rebecca, I was enrolled in college. I had already completed my first year, and since we met, I had completed another semester. When I lost my job, I was faced with a difficult decision—I could continue to go to school, or I could eat.

I guess that doesn't really sound like a difficult decision, does it?

I dropped out of school and continued to look for work in Long Beach and the surrounding cities. I was living in a friend's garage and sleeping on a couch. As time passed, our circumstances deteriorated. I felt like a loser, being out of work. Communication between Rebecca and me broke down. Just before the holidays, Rebecca said she needed some time to think again. We split up, and I fell into a deep depression.

Listening to my angel had been easy. Believing my angel when he said I would meet my soul mate had been easy. Making that relationship work, with the real world stresses of money, family, and personal history, was a lot more difficult.

During this time, my grandmother reached out to me and asked me if I wanted to go on a road trip. She and my grandfather had a camper, and she thought it would be fun to drive up to see my sister, who was living in Fresno with her boyfriend and her little boy. I wasn't crazy about the idea of spending time with my grandfather, another poor role model, but I liked the thought of spending time with my sister, whom I hadn't seen in a while. Everything was going badly where I was, so I agreed to go.

We arrived in Fresno. It was great to see my sister. Tina appeared to be happy, and it was a treat to see my nephew again—I hadn't seen him in a few years.

The next morning, after breakfast, when I thought we'd continue to catch up on old times, my angel told me to say, "I'm going for a walk, and I'll be back."

I did as I was told, and walked out of the house.

"Okay, I'm listening. Where to now?"

The voice said: *Just start walking.*

I walked through the neighborhood, the voice guided me through every turn. I found myself headed toward Fresno State University. As I passed the very large, beautiful, and state-of-the-art football stadium, my angel guided me into the campus.

The voice directed me to a residence hall. I walked into the kitchen and saw the chef chopping vegetables. I spoke with him and, upon the urging of my angel, I shared my story and told him I would love to work there. He liked that I had restaurant experience and he admired the fact that, instead of taking a vacation, I was out looking for a job on my first day in the area. He said he liked my tenacity and spunk, and I was hired on the spot. They only had part-time hours for me at the moment, but I could start right away. I got my schedule and headed out.

My angel said: *Good job, but we're not done yet.*

I continued to walk around the campus, with my angel telling me which turns to take. Soon, I arrived at a little café in the food service building. I went inside, met the food service manager, and proceeded to share my work experience and my story with him. Once again, I was hired. I had secured two jobs in one day and, between them, I would have a full-time schedule. The job at the residence hall started just a few days later, and the job at the food service building would start as soon as the holiday vacation break was over.

I headed back to my sister's house to share the great news with my family. Needless to say, they were surprised. My grandmother was worried about how she was going to tell my mother that I wasn't coming home, but my sister was in heaven. I stayed with Tina until I got my first paycheck, and then rented an apartment in the same complex. It was wonderful to be living close to my sister again.

I called Rebecca and told her I had a job, a new place, and a new attitude. I asked her if she'd had enough time to think. I told her, if she was ready, I wanted to invite her to move in with me. She was excited by the opportunity, and welcomed the chance to get away from her grandmother. We bought her a bus ticket, and she came to Fresno to be with me.

When Rebecca arrived, she applied at the residence hall and was able to get a part-time job. We were used to the Southern California cost of living, so the low rent and expenses in Fresno seemed like a dream come true. Over time, we filled our own sweet little apartment with furniture and everything else we needed.

Life was good. I had my sister and nephew close by, and we were having fun, partying, smoking pot, and hanging out with new friends, who we felt were good people.

By saying that, I'm giving you the idea that these were, in fact, *not* good people, but that's not really fair. Many of them were good at heart level, but surely not great role models for us. They were leading us by example, but ultimately introduced us to a new and dangerous life—the world of drugs—which would eventually send us both into a downward spiral.

Introduction to Drugs, Bartending, and a New Friend

The local drug of choice was crank, a low-cost form of speed. It was made locally from all kinds of nasty chemicals. Doing the drug made the user feel euphoric, and it helped with weight loss. Soon, we were regular users, but we were functional and feeling good. We thought we were doing well. I wanted to continue losing weight, so I regularly ran the bleachers at the football stadium. Life was good.

Eventually, the person who had been getting the drugs for us got tired of having to get it so often, so they made a direct introduction—to take out the middleman. When I started to meet with the dealer directly, I thought it was fantastic—now I could score pretty much anytime I wanted.

Once we got to know the dealer, it wasn't long before he invited us to stick around instead of scoring and leaving. We watched as he dissolved the crank with liquid in a spoon, sucked it up into a needle, tied off his arm, and shot himself up. He let the rubber arm tie loose and sat back to enjoy the ride. He didn't move or say a word for about ten minutes.

Having had a fear of needles since childhood, I'm not sure I would've ever tried it myself if Rebecca had not been with me. I closed my eyes, dealt with my fear, and went to another place once the needle came out. It was unlike anything I'd ever experienced and better than most. I loved it. Just like that, I was hooked.

We spent a lot of time at the guy's house. If we weren't working, we were shooting up. Somehow, we remained functional, probably because we wanted to keep doing the drug, and we needed money to do that. We paid our bills, but all other money went to this drug. We would mix it up with cocaine, or alcohol and cocaine, and on a good day, he would have some crystal meth. We were having a wonderful time in the land of no-cares-and-no-worries.

I continued to lose weight. My sister noticed that I was looking gaunt and unhealthy, and she told me she was concerned. I told her not to worry and that it wasn't any of her business anyway. Eventually she found out, pulled me aside, and confronted me. I denied using—the first time I'd ever lied to my sister.

Lying to Tina must have triggered a red flag inside me, warning me that I was on the wrong path, but I ignored it. I am certain that my angel gave me numerous hints that I also ignored, just as I ignored anything that suggested I shouldn't be doing drugs. The voice in my head was the drug now, and it seemed to have a much louder voice than my angel did. I had selective hearing, as the drug was slowly becoming my priority.

When the school year ended, Rebecca and I were laid off for the summer. They offered to let one of us stay on at the residence hall, but we felt it was best for us to look for other jobs. I got a job at a bar called Willikers, and worked my way up to assistant bartender from busboy. Eventually, Rebecca got a job at the same place. We continued to use.

At Willikers, the bar menu was a few hundred drinks deep, and the bartenders were trained to show off. They flipped glasses, spun shaker tins, and made the drinks in a fancy way to make the experience fun.

I was up for a promotion, but I didn't get along with the bar manager, and he tried to keep me from moving up. When the general manager gave me the promotion anyway, the bar manager resented it, and tried to get me to quit. He gave me the worst shifts and tried to undermine me at every turn. I learned over two hundred recipes and could pour alcohol with complete accuracy. With the help of Darby, a local bartending legend, I became a fantastic show bartender.

The bar manager, realizing that he couldn't make me quit, started trying to get me fired. He told our boss that he suspected me of stealing. During one busy afternoon, I skipped ringing in an order.

This order was one of the two complimentary drinks I was permitted to offer each shift. The general manager called me into his office, pulled out the long receipt that reported every drink I had made, and asked me where that drink was. I explained that, in the rush, I had just forgotten to key in the comp.

He didn't fire me, but he laid into me, and accused me of stealing. When he said he'd be *keeping an eye on me,* I told him where he could stick it. I didn't want to work where I wasn't trusted.

I was pissed off, but worse, I was out of a good-paying job. I walked down the main strip about a mile to another restaurant, called the Silver Dollar Hofbrau, and talked to the bar manager there. He sympathized, but didn't have a job for me.

As I sat there, feeling let down and jobless, I turned within and asked my angel: *What should I do next?*

I clearly heard my angel's voice say: *Sit there, and do what I tell you.*

Just then, the bartender who was scheduled to work the happy-hour shift called in sick.

I called the bar manager over and repeated what the voice told me to say: "I heard you say that your bartender called in sick for happy hour. I would be glad to fill in and help you out. I will work that shift with you, and if, by the end of that shift, you don't want to hire me full-time, you just let me know, and I will leave and never bother you again. But let me work this shift with you to show you what I can do."

He thought for a minute and agreed. The bar manager went back to his office and came back with a shirt for me. I put it on and stepped behind the bar. He showed me how to work the register, how the soda guns worked, where the beer mugs were, how to put in food orders, and gave me as much instruction as he could before the happy-hour crowd started to arrive.

We got slammed quickly. Although I was out of my element with the new physical arrangement, I had a calm and self-assured feeling inside. I knew I was going to do great. I tried out some of my show moves, flipping the beer mugs. Some were amused, some not so much. This was a blue-collar bar. These people didn't need fancy; they wanted speed. Noticing that, I kept it focused and moved as quickly as I could.

One customer offered an odd answer when I asked him what he would like.

He turned to the guy next to him and said, "He'll learn."

He ordered a Budweiser draft and a Christian Brothers brandy straight up. I couldn't understand why someone would be so rude, but I was too busy to give it much thought. When the man finished his drinks, I automatically got him another draft and brandy.

He looked at the guy next to them, chuckled, and said, "He learned."

I was still missing the joke, but I didn't have time to figure it out. I moved on to the next customer.

By the end of the night, I had mastered their system. The bar manager told me to change my shirt and have a seat on the other side of the bar. He bought me a drink, and after he got the next shift ready to go, he sat next to me and showed me the next week's bartenders' schedule.

He said, "You start tomorrow, you have five shifts per week. You are now a full-time bartender at the Silver Dollar. Welcome aboard!"

Once again, I had followed the voice of my angel, and everything had worked out.

Part II

Earthbound Angels

4

My New Friend John

The odd customer I had met on that first day working at The Silver Dollar Hofbrau was a regular at the bar. This man would make a lasting—lifetime—impression on me. He would teach me, support me, and completely alter the story of my life. For the telling of this story, I'll call him John.

I'd see John almost every day.

No matter what I asked him, he'd always initially respond, "You'll learn."

One night, I asked him if he'd like to hang out after work. I wanted to know what it was that he wanted me to learn.

John was a quiet person, but as we got to know each other, I realized he was actually a great storyteller. He seemed to have wisdom beyond his age.

One day, John told me the story of a child who had a great imagination, but had given it up to take care of his sick mother. When he was young, he'd had a strong bond with an angel, who talked with him and watched over him. The child had grown up, had forgotten what his purpose was, and came to shun his great powers.

He told me that this boy was visited by a guardian angel when he was in his twenties, and the angel took him to do things he never got to do as a child. He showed the boy miracles beyond human belief. The angel saved that boy's life and restored his faith. Once the boy, now a man, was on the right path, the angel left to save another soul from a life of sadness.

I said, "I can sure relate to that kid."

My friend laughed and said, "I'll bet you can."

We started to hang out regularly after work.

Adventures with John

One night John said, "I know you don't believe in psychics or fortune tellers. I know you don't believe in much. But do you trust me?"

I assured him I did.

He said, "Good. Let me see your ring."

He pointed to my stepfather Mel's wedding ring. My mother had given me the ring when I was old enough to be trusted with it. It was hard for me to hand it to anyone, but I did trust John, so I took it off and handed it to him.

He closed his fingers around the ring and shut his eyes. As he took a deep breath, I could tell something was happening. I watched his face. He smiled, he laughed, he got serious, and at one point, he twitched and made a horrific looking face. He opened his eyes, and handed me the ring. I could tell he was trying to shake off whatever he had seen.

When John finally spoke, he told me *my* story.

He started with my childhood and shared things about me that I had not told anyone. He said that he had seen Mel's death and had experienced it.

He shuddered and said, "I would have preferred to not see that part."

Then he smiled, and he told me my stepfather was still watching over me.

I was blown away.

I had learned to doubt everything over the last several years, but for the first time, I was rethinking that position. I admit, however, that soon after, I began to mistrust what he said.

Believing and trusting had become difficult for me. I'm not sure if it had to do with Rebecca, or the drugs, or perhaps it was something internal that was crying out for guidance in my young adult years. Likely, it was a combination of all these factors and more. I still believed in my guardian angel, but my level of confidence in everything else was horribly low.

John told me there was a reason we had met. There were things he needed to show me, things he needed to tell me, and that, one day, he would save my life. He told me not to worry about that day or even give it any more thought, but he wanted me to know that, once that day happened, he would be gone.

John could predict the future. He did it all the time. He showed me many things I had a hard time believing, even though I saw them with my own eyes. Often, he would have to demonstrate a phenomenon several times before I would let myself believe.

John was a model of persistence and patience. He did all that he could to prove to me that there was more to life than what I could see, but

I was, to say the least, a slow learner. Time after time, I would see extraordinary displays, but would dismiss them soon after.

There are no better words to describe what he did other than to say he was performing miracles.

John was constantly trying to show me how to trust myself and how to tune into my instincts. He had to show me proof repeatedly until finally, I believed. Once I did, he was able to show me how to do some of these things myself. When, finally, I believed in this man's power, when I realized he had been sent to teach me, it was then that he told me the truth about who he was. He was an *earthbound angel.*

He told me there were people on Earth who were here to do great works. If these people died, or were diverted from their true path due to bad choices, the world would be negatively affected. These people he referred to as *difference makers*. As hard as it was for me to believe, he counted me among them.

Earthbound angels were assigned to save the difference makers from themselves. They did whatever they could to befriend these people and to earn their trust enough so they could finally share the truth. He asked me again if I would trust him, if I could let down my guard of disbelief, and let him teach me. He warned that what I would experience might seem strange, or might not make sense to me, but everything he would do had a purpose and was in support of my higher good.

It was so hard to make this leap of faith. You might be wondering why I had such a tough time with this. I already had extensive experience with an angel, as you know. It would seem to follow that trusting in another angel would be easy for me.

Why was this leap of faith so much harder?

You may find it interesting to learn that, although I believed wholeheartedly in guardian angels, I had a hard time believing that there were angels *among us*—the earthbound angels in human form. My only explanation is that I had lived with a guardian angel for my entire life, but had never before been aware of earthbound angels.

In retrospect, maybe my reluctance had to do with the reality of John's human form. In my experience, humans were frail and fallible; not at all like my guardian angel, who never faltered.

I had a million questions of John. Only rarely did he give a direct answer. Every question was met with a question.

I used to feel like pulling my hair out, wondering: *Why won't he just answer me?*

I would eventually come to learn that it was all for my own good. There were times, however, when it would have been nice just to hear a *yes* or *no*!

Over the next year, I spent a lot of time with John. It was quite a series of adventures and I have shared some of them below.

The Cave

One day, John and I drove out to the middle of nowhere, parked his truck, and then hiked for a little while. Soon we arrived at what looked like a hole in the ground. As had become my habit, I followed John. We went a few steps down into the cave, and he reached into his backpack and pulled out a flashlight. Soon there was no light at all, except for the flashlight that John had in his hands.

After we were in the cave for about a half an hour, John was about a hundred feet in front of me. I needed to catch up since I couldn't see much ahead; I was relying on his flashlight. Suddenly the light went out, and I learned the meaning of not being able to see my hand in front of my face. I called out to John.

There was no response.

I started to feel intense anxiety and fear. I started hyperventilating. I remembered my mother and her claustrophobia—I always thought she was exaggerating how bad she felt. Now I was experiencing it myself, and I was able to understand the panic she went through.

Where did John go?

Why did the flashlight turn off, and why would he leave me?

My heart raced, and I was about to lose it when I heard John's voice say, "Breathe, take a breath, relax, and trust. Don't worry."

He told me to sit down on the ground cross-legged, and he repeated that I should take a nice deep breath, relax, and trust.

I did as instructed. My heartbeat slowed, and the anxiety subsided, I focused on my breathing, and before I knew it, I was calm. When I was relaxed again, the flashlight came back on. John was standing in the exact spot where he had been when the flashlight went off. He had not moved. I could have simply walked a hundred feet, and I would have bumped into him, but instead, I had freaked out.

He explained this was a metaphor for life. There would be many times in my life when I would become accustomed to walking in the light, then something would happen, and the light would appear to dim or turn off. How I reacted in these situations would determine my ability to survive them. The way I reacted would also determine how much I would be able to learn from my life experiences.

He told me to think of it this way: *The light is always just a hundred feet away.*

The light never leaves; it only appears to. When this happens in life, you have a choice. You can freak out, get anxious, get depressed, blame the light, point fingers, struggle, and judge—or you can trust that the light is still there.

If you can know in your heart that the light is still there, all you need to do is stay calm, and navigate your way forward until you find the light.

I would like to say that, after this experience, a door opened, and I understood all of this.

Alas, it wasn't so. To tell you the truth, when John was talking to me, I was still suffering from the effects of my panic and didn't quite get it. As I said, he had to repeat many of his lessons for me before they would sink in.

Eventually, I would come to understand the profundity of his message, but, at that moment, I was still mad at him.

Grapevine Driving

When I was a teenager, I had a traumatic experience as a passenger in a pickup truck, not unlike my night with Timar. We were both drunk and he was speeding through the town, running lights, sliding turns, barely missing hitting solid objects. At first, it was fun, but after a few close calls, I started thinking about pedestrians, children, animals—or us—ending up dead. How we lived through that night, I'll never know. I had nightmares about it for years afterward.

John drove a big truck. One night he pulled off into a field of grapevines, which are everywhere in Fresno. Just like when I was teenager, we were speeding through the grapevines, zigzagging, and doing crazy sliding turns.

The difference was that now, I was with John, so I knew everything was going to be all right. Having him in the driver's seat somehow reframed my earlier experience, allowing me to relax, and let my residual fear dissipate. In effect, it freed me from the anxiety that had persisted inside me all those years. Plus, I got to enjoy being on a wild ride, like in the movies, without incident.

This was the start of what John would do with a lot of my negative childhood memories. I would be given the chance to revisit, reexamine, and reframe them. I would eventually come to understand what an incredibly valuable gift this was.

The River

One sunny day, John took me down to a little river in the middle of nowhere in the San Joaquin Valley. We hiked around, talked, shared stories, and connected. When the sun got low, John gathered twigs, branches, and larger pieces of wood. He had some newspaper in the back of his truck, so he had everything necessary to build a fire.

As the sun got lower, I kept waiting for him to light the fire, but he didn't. John suggested I get my guitar, which I had brought along. I took it out of the case and started playing. Before the sunset ended in darkness, John grabbed a flare and walked out almost to the other side of the Little River. He lit the flare and stuck it into the shallow riverbed. About half of the flare was sticking out of the water creating the coolest looking red glow in and around the water. It's hard to explain, but it was beautiful.

I was looking at the flare and playing the guitar when John told me, "Look into the light. Notice the color and the power of the fire. Look at the reflection in the water. See how it moves, shifts, has waves that give the appearance of constant movement. Look into the light. Breathe. Look into the light. Breathe. Look into the light, and play."

I was in a trance. I felt connected to the earth, to the fire, to the water, and to the light. I started playing, and a song poured out of me in its entirety, fully written from beginning to end. Strangely, the song included chords that I had never before played on the guitar. And I was playing them without looking at the guitar. It was as though the music was playing itself. When the song finished, I kind of shook my head and snapped out of it.

I looked at John and said, "What was that?"

John just smiled and said, "Looks like you have a new song."

Amazingly, I remembered every chord. I have since recorded the song, and, until recently, it was the only instrumental song I had in my repertoire.

Patience

During my precious time with John, he brought me from not believing in anything to believing in *everything*. As an earthbound angel, John knew I would need to do some of these extraordinary things myself in order to truly believe them. There was a long period where it seemed like I was in training. It was like Mr. Miyagi teaching in *The Karate Kid*.

John helped me to harness some special powers for limited periods. There were times when I got to do supernatural acts myself. Still, my doubts persisted, although I tried not to let them in. There were times when I saw things that were out of this world, and, by the next day, I would think I had made it all up. John was so patient with me that I used to joke with him by calling him Job.

One day, John did something he considered a small thing, but I was totally blown away. In response, he looked up to the heavens as if in complete frustration.

He exclaimed, "He's impressed by my parlor tricks!"

He brought his eyes back down to me, kind of shaking his head.

He said, "If you only knew the power you have, you would hardly be impressed by anything that I can do. I look forward to the day you own your power. On that day, the student will become the master."

Calzone

Seeing is believing. Believing is seeing. One night, John, Rebecca, and I were hanging out, and having fun. I got hungry, took out some leftover calzone, put it on a cookie sheet, and stuck it in the oven. I came back into the living room and forgot about it. It was quite a while later when I remembered the calzone. I knew it had been in the oven long enough so it would be crispy black—if not on fire—in the oven. I grabbed the potholders, opened up the oven, pulled out the pan, and saw that the calzone was perfectly cooked. It looked delicious.

My mind quickly remembered how long it'd been since I put it in the oven, and I thought, "This doesn't make sense at all. This can't be right."

No sooner did I finish the sentence than the calzone burst into flames and turned into a crispy pile of burnt food.

John called from the other room, "You had it all. It was perfectly cooked. You created a miracle, but then you doubted it. You doubted yourself, and how did that work out for you? Now you don't have any dinner."

I was ashamed that I had let myself down once again. I had seen greater things than a calzone not burning in the oven, but still I doubted. I was so keyed in to disbelief that it just took over sometimes.

That day, John told me, "There is no time and space. It doesn't really exist. It's something man made up so he could show up to work when expected, to show up for friends when requested. It's an earthly measurement, but the truth is, in reality, it does not exist. There is no forward, there is no backward, there is no yesterday, there is no tomorrow; there's only right now. What you choose in each moment dictates the next moment. Manifestation can be instantaneous, as you just demonstrated so profoundly. As soon as you thought: *This can't be right,* it wasn't.

Think back to all the times you have wished for something or said something would come true, and you believed it. How many of those things came true? For you, they've come true more often than for most, and still you don't believe. Come on, Keith. Get this. There is no time and space—it doesn't really exist."

Turning the Power off on a City Block

John told me I would be allowed to control the elements. I didn't know what he meant by that. He told me to get creative and figure it out.

At the time, I was a sales manager for a training and marketing company, and Rebecca was the office manager. Because of all the work I'd been doing with John, I found it hard to stay focused at my job. One day, I was complaining to Rebecca, and she suggested I do something about it. I asked her what she meant.

She said, "John said you had command of the elements, so do something."

I thought, "Well, we wouldn't be able to work if we didn't have electricity."

I ran it by Rebecca and she said, "Go for it."

I closed my eyes and imagined being able to do something like that.

I allowed myself to believe in what I could do, and then commanded, "Electricity—turn off."

And it did, immediately.

We looked at each other and said, "Wow."

It was completely dark. Laughing in disbelief as we left, we noticed other people were coming out of their buildings and offices as well.

When we asked what was going on, someone told us, "The power is out."

There were people standing in front of their offices scratching their heads, and the traffic light on the corner of the block was out as well. I had turned off the electricity for a whole city block.

"I guess I should be more specific," I said, and we laughed out loud.

Once I stopped laughing at the wonder of it all, I started doubting myself—again. I decided I should turn the electricity back on, since others needed it to work. I closed my eyes and tried. Of course, nothing happened. I said all the right words, but my doubts, once again, were getting in the way.

It was a long drive home. One part of me was excited at what I had done, and the other part was disappointed about what I hadn't been able to do. When we arrived home, I told our roommate, Maria, what happened. She suggested since I had learned the lesson that needed to be learned, I should try again.

I commanded out loud, "Electricity, turn back on in the city block of our workplace."

I called our workplace neighbors and confirmed that the electricity had come back on, including the traffic lights. I was relieved, but only temporarily. By the next day, I didn't believe any of it had happened. I believed in John, but had yet to fully believe in myself.

Telekinesis

One of the more mind-blowing experiences with John involved telekinesis. For a full day, I could move anything with my mind. I started with a pencil, moving it on the table back and forth. Then I remembered seeing some magician doing the spoon bending trick and thought I would try it for myself. I grabbed the spoon and held it. I visualized the spoon handle melting in my hand, and the spoon bent. I dropped it on the table and scooted back in shock.

I experimented throughout the day. For some reason—even though for most people this one might have been the hardest one for them to wrap their mind around—I had no problem with telekinesis.

Perhaps I was starting to believe.

Only time would tell.

Don't Speak for Two Weeks

Rebecca and I had several roommates over the years. One of them, Ken, was the most egotistical, obnoxiously loud, constantly-needing-to-be-right person I'd ever met. He had enough energy for three people. He made me seem quiet by comparison.

At this point in my life, cocaine was my drug of choice. I no longer had a crank connection. I was off the needle, so I thought I was doing better. Ken was a dealer and dealt drugs from the house. As addicts ourselves, we didn't mind.

You can imagine what living in this apartment was like; the people who came and went, the parties that happened, and the senseless ramblings of addicts arguing about anything and everything. Addicts and dealers—it wasn't a great mix. Ken talked all the time, and John, who would come over and sit on the couch not saying a word, was always looking at me and shaking his head.

John made Ken very uncomfortable.

He would ask, "What the hell is that guy's problem? Why won't he say anything?"

I said, "You just have to get to know him before he'll talk to you. He is a man of few words."

Ken replied, "How does he not know me? He's here every night. He just sits there and stares at us and doesn't say a word."

I was irritated by his incessant grumbling and finally said, "Why don't you ask him your own damn self?"

So, he did.

In response to Ken's angry questions, John said, "First of all, if there was ever a conversation happening that was worth commenting on, I would comment. Second, I don't speak just to speak. Lastly, you can learn more from listening than you can from talking. You might want to try it sometime."

His last sentence was spoken with great authority.

Immediately after this, John, Rebecca, and I left the party and went out.

John said, "I have your next mission, should you choose to accept it. You are not allowed to speak for the next two weeks. If there is an emergency and you need to speak to help yourself or someone else, that is the exception. In addition, when you're at work, you can talk. Other than those two scenarios, you will not speak. If you're willing to do this, you will gain a complete understanding of what I just told your friend. Truly, you can learn more from listening than you can from talking. Will you do it?"

I agreed.

I could write a whole book about those two weeks of my life. Watching and observing my roommate, his friends, and clients interact with each other was enlightening. I found that even when I was bartending, I could do a lot of listening. This was a big change for me because I do love to hear myself talk, and I enjoy involving myself in conversations.

One night, Ken and this other guy were arguing over something for well over an hour. What they were talking about was completely insignificant, but they were both stuck in their position, and each had a tremendous need to be right. No matter who came and joined the conversation, nothing changed. There was so much talking going on, and absolutely no listening. At one point, I looked at both of them and shook my head in disbelief.

Ken looked at me and said, "Well, what do you think?"

This was the only moment in the two weeks that I broke my silence outside of work. As John had so many times, I spoke what I believed to be the truth about the situation in one sentence. Then I went back into the silence.

Ken and the guy looked at each other and totally agreed with what I had said.

Ken asked, "If you knew the answer the whole time, why did you just sit there and let us argue for hours about this?"

I shrugged and stayed silent. As if they would have listened to me.

Those two weeks were the longest, but most profound, of my life. Here's some of what I learned:

- A lot of people speak, but very few are willing to listen.
- It's rare that people get to finish speaking their truth without being interrupted.
- People tend to plan their next reply long before the other person has finished.
- People put up walls to keep others from seeing who they really are.
- Right or wrong is just an opinion and cannot be proven.
- Political arguments are a complete waste of time and energy.
- People will tell you what they need if you're willing to listen.
- I gained compassion for people who command constant attention.
- I don't want to be a person who commands constant attention.
- I forgave myself for all the times I commanded constant attention.
- As John had predicted, I learned more from listening than I did from talking.

The Journey

At some point, something shifted inside me. I stopped asking stupid questions and started to believe the profundity of the lessons I was being taught.

When this shift occurred, John told me, "It's time for you to take a journey."

John handed me his mini screwdriver, which he always carried, and instructed me to wear a shirt with a pocket, and put the screwdriver in there when I went to sleep. The screwdriver needed to stay with me. It was important that it was something that John constantly had on his person. The possession of the screwdriver was about fostering energy exchange—what I now know as *energy connections*. The mini screwdriver would allow us to maintain contact.

That night, I did as I was told. I had the mini screwdriver on me as I drifted off to sleep. It didn't seem like much time had passed before I raised up out of my body and was floating, looking down at myself while I slept. This was not a dream. I knew that at any time I could jump right into my body and wake up. Actually, I had never felt as *awake* as I did in that moment.

A few seconds later, John appeared next to me, looking as he always did.

He said, "Are you ready for your journey?"

I replied, "This isn't it?"

He grinned and answered, "This is just the beginning, my friend."

I said, "I'm as ready as I'll ever be."

He said, "We're about to go to a place far, far away. Hold onto my hand, and trust me."

We continued to float upwards through the ceiling into the sky, and then we just took off. The next part was straight out of a Peter Pan movie. It was beautiful. I had been able to fly in many of my dreams before, but this did not feel like a dream at all. There was nothing but beautiful lights, with houses and grapevines below. It wasn't long before we were soaring over mountains. Everything was illuminated by the light of the moon and stars. We continued to a place that looked very much like the desert. It was dark, but the hills and valleys were smooth and glistening from sand.

I noticed a big fire down below with many figures sitting around it. We slowly floated towards the pit and took our seats around the large crackling fire.

There were many figures around the fire, few of whom I can remember specifically. Some of them were human figures, but there were also a variety of manifested shapes—what I refer to as *avatars*. One was an old Indian man, with deep wrinkles on his face and a river of ancient wisdom deep in his eyes. There was another old man, who looked to be of Middle Eastern descent and had the look of a dark-skinned Jesus. One avatar had no shape at all; it was just colors of swirling light.

I don't remember much of what was said, because at the time I was not able to understand what I heard. Mostly I remember feeling loved, trusted, and guided. All questions I asked were answered, but mostly I listened. I was told what my purpose in this lifetime was, exactly what I was here to do while I am on this earth, when I would do these things, and how I would do them.

It seemed like we were there for hours. Yet before I knew it, it was time to leave. John once again took my hand, and we rose above the fire into the sky and journeyed back home, flying over the desert, over the cascading mountains, over the city of lights, the house, through the roof and ceiling, and to my body, still sleeping soundly below.

I knew this was no dream.

John said, "It's time for me to leave now. I will see you later today, and you can tell me about this experience when we are both back in our bodies."

After he left, I hovered above my body. I drifted downward slowly and stopped about a foot from my sleeping self. I took time to look closely at myself. I studied each hair, and listened to my breath. I saw myself, in that moment, for the beautiful person I was—the beautiful person I *am*. I felt an unconditional love for myself that I had never experienced before, and when I was ready, I floated back into my body. I immediately woke up, and I sat in my bed, smiling, knowing it was as real as anything I had ever experienced before, probably more so.

When I met up with John the next day, he asked me what I remembered. I told him I remembered our flight together and arriving at the big fire.

I said, "I know I received guidance and my life purpose, but I don't remember any details."

I told him I was puzzled about this.

John said, "Oh, you're not ready for all that yet. If you remembered it all, it would probably make your head explode. You were told all the steps you will take, and the ways you will live into your purpose. You were given a glimpse in the future about all the people whose lives you will touch in the process. You were given specific instructions, and when you need to know them, the memories of their instruction will come to you vividly. You'll receive these instructions in your dream state and while you're awake. When you receive information, you will remember being at that fire, so you'll know the instructions came from that meeting. In other words, visions will come to you on an as-needed basis. Just follow the instructions as they come, and the way to achieve what you're told will be provided. You're up to something big here. You'll see."

As the years passed, it happened just as John had told me it would. I had dreams and visions, and afterwards, I could write down the memories and record the instructions from this out of body experience. One of my visions included my life purpose in its entirety. I guess I was ready for the information, which came to me with many details about what I would do for my business, books I would write, campaigns I would undertake—all of it leading to this book.

I was told I would write a book called *Walking with My Angels.*

I was told to wait for an angel voice to tell me when to begin.

This book has a specific purpose and it's no accident you have it in your hands right now.

Ninja Lessons in the Park

John, being in earthbound angel, had some hobbies to keep him busy. He had fun when he was not at his income-earning job or being of service to others like me.

John was also a ninja.

A ninja?

Yeah, I didn't expect that either.

I always thought ninjas were a legend, or something that only Asian people practiced in the past. I had no idea there were people practicing this art worldwide. When John told me that, in his free time, he was a practicing ninja, I didn't know what that meant, or what kind of practice was involved.

One night, John asked Rebecca and me if we wanted to experience his ninja playground.

We did, of course.

He instructed us to wear all black and to be ready at midnight for him to pick us up. We dressed accordingly. He showed up on time dressed in black himself, and we drove quite a while to a forest that I had only heard of before. I had never been there myself and neither had Rebecca. We were both excited.

When we arrived, he told us the rules. The first was to be as silent as we could be. The second was not to be scared of anything we saw or heard. The third rule was follow his directions, which would be visual cues, not verbal words. Next, he did his best to teach two rookies how to walk, with leaves underfoot, without being heard. Ninjas must master this, as their goal is to be neither heard nor seen. We got the concept, but neither of us was very good at it. I'm sure it takes years to develop that ability. We did understand he was trying to teach us something valuable so we could be part of the experience.

He told us to follow him, not be scared, and most of all, to have fun. He told us there were others there to practice also, and that everyone was there to have fun—nobody would hurt us, nobody wanted to scare us, and anything that happened was in good fun. Ninjas would be all around us, and our goal was to see them or discover them. Nobody would touch us. If we could actually see them on our first time here, we'd be ahead of most people.

Finally, he told us it was time for him to stop talking. He waved us on as if to say *follow me*. We stood there as he walked off without making a sound. Rebecca and I were already very surprised. We tried our best, but there were definitely leaves crackling under our feet. We smiled and tried to snicker as quietly as we could as we followed him into the woods.

Approximately a hundred yards into the woods, we saw what looked to be a pile of leaves. John snuck up on the pile and touched it. When he did, a black figure popped out and took off into the woods without making a sound. It was another person in a ninja suit who was completely invisible until John touched him. He continued into the woods without making a sound as we lagged behind.

We watched as he walked up to a tree, reached around, and touched something.

We heard someone say, "Ahhhhh."

Again, a black figure took off from behind the tree and disappeared quickly. It looked like a game of tag. They were doing their best to become invisible in the woods. There were times when it felt like there were people all around us. We could sense them and we knew they were there, but we couldn't see any of them.

John had stayed in our sight up until this point, probably to make sure that we didn't get scared. When he thought we were comfortable, he vanished. It was our turn to try to find him. We searched around and touched piles of leaves, but they were only piles of leaves. We didn't find anyone, but it was fun trying.

A few minutes later we heard some leaves crackle about twenty feet in front of us, so we quickly hurried over to where we heard the sound and searched. We found nothing. Then we heard another crackling from a different direction, so we hurried and searched around. Once again, we came up empty-handed. This happened repeatedly. We were starting to feel like yo-yo's, going back-and-forth, up-and-down, and round-and-round.

Then we heard John laughing. We looked and found him, sitting cross-legged on the ground with a pile of rocks in front of him. He had been toying with us. He'd been sitting there all along, throwing a rock to the left, then one to the right, then one to the left, then one to the right, watching us go back-and-forth like two idiots in the woods.

It's a good thing he told us ahead of time that this was all in fun. Boy, did we feel silly.

He took us around, having fun identifying other people, scaring the crap out of them, and watching them disappear into the woods. I can see why he enjoyed it so much. Sometime before dawn, he pointed to the car, and we headed out of the woods.

As we drove home, we swapped stories and asked him questions about the game. He really got a kick out of hearing our version of being used like a human yo-yo when we were running back and forth searching for him. Seeing some of his abilities in action and being included in the fun made it a very special night.

Never Ask What You Don't Want to Know

I'm sure you've heard the expression: *Never ask a question if you don't really want to know the answer.*

Hanging out with John and learning all we were learning, Rebecca and I had many questions. Most times John answered a question with another question.

One night Rebecca looked at John and asked him, "When you had Keith's ring on and you saw his whole life, did you also see his future?"

I didn't expect him to answer directly, but he surprised me by saying, "Yes, I did."

She asked, "When you saw Keith's future, was I there with him?"

John responded, "You know I cannot answer that question, so why do you ask me?"

"I want to know—no, actually, I need to know," Rebecca said.

John replied, "Do not ask questions you really don't want to know the answer to. Besides, nothing that I saw has to mean anything. Reality can change at any time, by making one different decision. That is why people are given visions of the future. It enables us to be aware of the possibilities. Anything I see and tell you can be changed, so it has no significance in this moment, or in this moment, or this moment."

Again, she repeated, "When you had the ring in your hand and you saw Keith's future, was I there with him?"

"You really want to know?" John asked.

"Yes, yes, I do."

And John replied, "No, you were not there."

After receiving her answer, Rebecca said, "You see, I told you someday you'll leave me just like my father did."

I wasn't surprised when she stormed out of the room. We both had abandonment issues. After that night, she pretended to shrug it off. I knew, however, it had deeply affected her. Things were never the same between her and John after that.

It was also a piece of information I didn't know what to do with.

5

My Time With Larry Wright

After I left my job as sales manager for the training and marketing company, I started working at a car lot. The first person I got to know was a man named Larry Wright. Larry was about five feet four inches tall, thin, and appeared to be a little older than I was. His eyes were deep blue, and his energy was calm and collected. We worked a high stress sales job, but no matter what the day held, this man always embodied a love of life.

At this time in my life, due in large part to the drugs I was using, the timeline of what took place is a bit unclear. The events themselves, however, are vivid in my mind.

Early in the day, all the salesmen would line up across the car lot and wait for people to come to test-drive cars. Larry and I spent hours talking while we waited. In between customers, we shared stories about our lives. I felt like I could say anything to Larry, and I did. I talked to him about the life-altering experiences I was having with the earthbound angel, John. These experiences were still brand-new to me, and I was struggling with the new beliefs. Larry listened and didn't seem fazed at all. He was the only person besides Rebecca with whom I could share my experiences of working with John.

Larry felt like an old soul. I imagined he had been here many times before and he was very aware of his experiences. It felt like there was nothing I could tell him that he hadn't already seen—or could imagine.

Larry spoke in a soft voice, almost a whisper. Many times, I had to lean in to hear him speak. He was a wise man and was willing to share his knowledge with me. He talked a lot about being used by God. He had been instructed to do certain things, some that made sense to him, and some that did not.

He used to say, "Mine is not to wonder why. I just do what I'm told."

This way of being was starting to make sense to me.

Larry was another person who could manifest his word, and he could do it at lightning speed. I used to call him *Zapper*. He would say something and, just like that, it would come true.

Standing in the car lot, he would say, "God, let the next person who comes on the lot be drawn to me. Let us be an energetic match, and if it is your will, let them buy a beautiful, fully-loaded car from me, at full price, with no haggling."

This sounded ridiculous because nobody bought a car without haggling. Sure enough, the next person who walked on the lot would walk straight over to him, introduce themselves, and the next thing I knew, they would be driving off in a beautiful car, fully loaded, having paid full price.

No Gas in the Pinto

Larry and I started hanging out after work. Night by night, if I wasn't with John, I was with Larry.

Larry had an old Ford Pinto car. It was comical that someone working at a car lot filled with brand-new cars would drive up in an ugly, beat-up, 1978 Pinto every day. This ugly car, however, never broke down. It seemed as if it were running without effort. The interior was comfortable. It was a dark green color, which matched the outside of the car. Everything about that car was green.

Although the car ran fine, the gas gauge didn't work. It was always on empty, and I never saw Larry stop at a gas station.

I once asked Larry, "If your gas gauge is broken, how do you know when it's time to fill up the car?"

He just smiled at me and drove.

I continued, "Seriously though, I've never seen you stop to get gas. How do you know when it's time?"

He looked at me and said, "God is my gasoline. I don't need gas to drive. I just need faith."

Larry had a great sense of humor, and I wondered if he was joking. I started to say something, and then decided to be quiet and just listen.

He continued, "I haven't filled this car up with gas in over a month. I haven't been making much money at the car lot. One day, when I didn't have enough money for gas, I prayed and asked what I should do. I was told not to worry about it, that God would keep my car running if I just had the faith of a mustard seed. That's what I've been doing ever since. God is my gasoline, God is my power, God is my source, and with God all things are possible."

I still wasn't sure if he was making this up, but we never did stop for gas.

Larry was full of divine wisdom. He was a walking soundbite. I wish I had written down all the things he said. His words made me wonder. They filled me with hope, and were usually complementary to what I was learning with John.

Between Larry and John, my consciousness was getting an intense workout every day. It was an amazing time. Work and sleep were academic at this point. All I could think about was spending time with my mentors.

Fortunately, Rebecca was as interested in these things as I was, so I could share them with her. She knew by then that I was here for a purpose and that all of this was happening for a reason. She tried never to stand in the way of my learning with John and Larry.

My two mentors were similar in some ways, as you have seen, but they worked differently in my life. The time I spent with John was all about teaching and learning. He was the master, and I was the student. Everything we did together was geared to take me from disbelief to belief.

In contrast, with Larry, the lessons were all about living in the moment. He was divinely guided, and I could feel this when I was with him. When he heard a voice or had a vision, he acted upon it, without reservation, without doubt or worries. He just did what he was told and knew that everything would work out, no matter what. Being in the moment with him was an intense joy. There were no limits to what I could do or be.

Crash at the Car Lot

I was working at the car lot one Saturday morning, when something happened that was a turning point in my life. As was typical, we were waiting for potential customers to pull into the lot, and hoping to make some sales. Larry was off that day, so I was standing by myself, facing the street.

I stood there kind of in a trance, just spinning Mel's ring on my finger. Watching the traffic, my attention was caught by a motorcycle speeding down the congested street. A minivan, with a family inside, stopped abruptly in front of the motorcycle. I could see that the motorcyclist was looking at the car lot instead of the road.

My heart was in my throat: *He doesn't see the minivan.*

My next thought was of Mel, and I was gripped by an old feeling of terror.

Do you remember that my stepfather, Mel, died in a horrible motorcycle accident?

I flashed back on my stepfather's accident, and when I came back to the present, the motorcyclist's brakes locked up, and he skidded toward the back of the minivan. His tire hit the back bumper.

I saw him fly through the back window, breaking the glass.

I heard children screaming, and I screamed out loud, "No!"

As soon as I screamed, time *reversed.*

I saw the man moving backwards. It looked as though he got spit out the back of the van. The broken glass became whole, and the man pushed off the back of the van and landed on his feet to the right of the van in the street.

He sat down on the curb, looking terrified.

Wild-eyed, he yelled, shaking his head, "No, no, no—no way!"

He looked around and then, still shaking his head, he said, "That *did not* just happen."

He had experienced that reversal of time, and was trying to make sense of it. I looked around at the other salesmen on the lot.

Were any of them watching? Had anyone else seen what I had?

One man named Carl, who was a devout Christian, looked at me, and said, "I saw what you did. You stay away from me," and he bolted toward the office.

After talking with people over the next few hours, it became apparent that none of the other salesmen had seen the accident and the reversal of time. Only Carl, the man on the motorcycle, and the people in the minivan had seen what I had.

The man on the motorcycle was near hysterical. He apologized repeatedly to the family. I heard him comparing notes with the minivan driver. Each of them had heard glass breaking, and had experienced the blood, the pain, and the death. All of them recalled the accident, followed by the sequence of events reversing before their eyes.

The police on scene assured them they were in shock, and that, eventually, they would realize they had all experienced a near miss and nothing more. Nobody could explain why everyone had heard breaking glass, yet the back window was unbroken. Nobody could explain why there was no damage to the van, but the bike was totaled.

I was kind of freaked out. I had seen time reverse when I was a teenager in the car crash with my friend, Timar, but that was a very long time ago. This time, it was significantly different.

This time, I was certain that *my will* had saved the lives of five people. It was a lot to wrap my brain around. I somehow got through my shift. Carl avoided me all day. Toward the end of the day, I went into the bathroom. Carl was there, and he wanted to talk.

He said, "I saw what you did. What was that? What happened? It was like a miracle, but why did it happen? Why did it happen like that?"

I shared the story of how my stepfather had been killed in a motorcycle accident and told him of my deep fear of motorcycles. I told him I had many experiences over the years with angels. I told him that everything his Savior, Jesus, had said was true; I had learned that the spoken word was creation. I told him we were in co-creation with the universe just as Jesus had claimed. I told him I could not explain why it had happened, but I was so glad that it had.

My eyes teared up as I told him, "I don't need to know how or why—I'm just so grateful right now."

Carl looked at me and said, "You're something else. That was crazy what I saw. But I did see it with my own two eyes. I cannot deny it. If God put you here to do that, then you're something else. You're all right with me. But we probably shouldn't be telling anybody else about it, or they will lock us both up and throw away the key."

I agreed, and we never mentioned it again.

When I returned home from work that night, I found John and Rebecca waiting for me.

John said, with a smirk on his face, "So, how was work today?"

I walked through the whole story without missing a detail.

When I finished, John looked into my eyes and asked, "Do you believe what you saw? Do you believe you had something to do with it? Do you now believe what I said about there not being any space or time? I guess the ultimate question is, do you believe?"

This time, I was able to answer with a very clear *"YES."*

The Funeral

On yet another day at the car lot, all the salesmen were on the line, standing and waiting for customers, when I noticed that one of our friends, Ted Riley, looked sad. As I was looking at him, his eyes had started to well up with tears. I asked him what was wrong.

He turned his head sideways and replied, "My grandmother died this morning. She meant the world to me. She helped raise me. I loved her, and she was my everything."

I said, "I'm so sorry, Ted. Is there anything I can do?"

He asked if Larry and I would come to the funeral. We agreed.

I had never been comfortable at funerals. Even seeing funerals in movies freaked me out. Just the thought of being around a dead body made me very uncomfortable.

I asked Larry why he thought Ted asked us to join him, and Larry said, "There must be some reason you were asked to be there. Maybe it's as simple as supporting Ted on one of the hardest days in his life. Who knows why? We were both instructed to say yes, so sitting around wondering why isn't going to do anyone any good. Let's show up, and see what happens."

I agreed, and we made our plans to be there for Ted at the funeral the next day.

Larry picked me up in the green machine. We wore the suits we wore every day. As we drove to the funeral, I shared my mixed emotions with Larry. Again, Larry assured me there was some divine purpose for us being asked to go, and I should relax.

The funeral was a graveside service. When Larry and I arrived, Ted was one of the first people we saw. We gave him a big hug, he introduced us to a few people, and we took our seats. Larry and I sat in silence as we watched the rest of the people arrive.

It was a very sweet and fairly short service. I could tell that each person who spoke about this woman loved her deeply. Two men of religion led the service: a Catholic priest and a Protestant minister. I thought it was pretty cool that there were two different religious energies present at this event. The closer we got to the end of the service, the greater the sadness became, as people realized that this was their last chance for closure. They all wanted a last chance to let her know how much they loved her.

As soon as the service was complete, I received my first instruction from an angel's voice. My instructions were odd, but I just did what I was told. The voice told me to pick up a rose, go over to the casket, pull off twelve petals, one at a time, and place them on the casket. Remarkably, nobody was paying any attention to me while I did this.

I completed my task, and shrugged my shoulders, thinking: *I don't know what that was about.*

Then, I remembered Larry's words: *There must be some reason you were asked to be there.*

As I turned away from the casket, I saw the line where all the family members were standing, and the people who attended the funeral started to move from one end to the other, hugging each family member until they had hugged each of them.

I jumped in the back of the line, wondering: *What am I doing in this line?*

It was hard to watch. Each family member was crying deeply. Some of them were trembling and shaking. I had never seen so much sadness in a group of people. The closer I got to the beginning of the hug line, the faster my heart beat.

I met the first family member, and said, "I'm sorry for your loss."

I gave her a hug. As I held her in my arms, I felt a wave of sadness come over me.

I moved on to the next family member, and said, "I'm sorry for your loss."

As I hugged this family member, the sadness inside of me grew immensely. The next family member was Ted.

I looked him in the eyes and said, "I'm sorry for your loss, Ted."

As I hugged him, my eyes watered, and tears filled my face. It was as if all his sadness had poured into me. I moved on to the next family member. It was a woman, and she was crying hysterically. She was breathing erratically. I hesitated, and then hugged her anyway. As I hugged her, again, I felt all her sadness move from her body into mine, and I started breathing the way she was breathing, gasping and weeping.

I continued to go from person to person, and with each hug, their sadness transferred to me. With each person, with each hug, my sadness grew. As the hugs went on, darkness started to fall upon me, until everything felt like it was closing in, and I was starting to have tunnel vision. By the time I finished with the last family member, I had almost blacked out. But Larry was standing right there with his hand out.

He grabbed my arm, put an arm around me as if to hold me up, and said, "Come with me—quickly."

As we headed toward his car, I looked back to the line of family members, and remarkably, each of them now had a big smile on their face. They joyously embraced each person in the hug line. All their sadness was gone. There was nothing but joy and love exuding from each family member.

Then things became dark again.

Larry sat me in the passenger seat of his car. He closed the door and quickly ran around to the driver seat and closed the door. Immediately, he started praying.

> *Lord God, I ask that you release Keith. He's done what you asked him to do. He has freed the family of their burdens, he has freed them of their pain, he took it all inside of him, and now it's time to let it out. Clear Keith's body of the other people's energy. Restore him, cleanse him, free him, and fill him with the light of your love, right now. I command this right now in the name of Jesus Christ. Lord God, make it so. Thank you God, Amen.*

As soon as he said *Amen*, the tunnel vision opened, and the sadness, the worry, the fear, and the pain of the family members subsided. I was filled with light. I began to feel joyful, happy, and grateful. Larry told me to take deep breaths, and to let each breath fill me with God's love. I was so grateful to have him there for me. I wouldn't have known what to do. I'm quite sure I would've passed out.

"Thank you, Larry," I said.

"No problem. Great work, brother," Larry replied, and we sat in silence.

After a time of silence, we noticed it was time for the funeral procession to head for the reception.

I turned to Larry and said, "Do we have to go?"

He laughed and replied, "Of course we do. We are here for Ted."

As we pulled up to the house where the reception held, we noticed that every family member was still smiling. The room was filled with love and joy. Larry and I were greeted with a big hug from Ted. He thanked us for coming, and told us how much he appreciated us being there for him. The food was good, and the company was great. We didn't really know anyone, but we were enjoying connecting with each person.

Larry and I walked outside to the back of the house by the pool. We were standing next to each other, eating, when the Catholic priest walked by. He looked at Larry, and then looked at me.

Once our eyes made contact, his eyebrows went up, and he said, "I know you. We've met before, right?"

I said, "I don't think so."

He said, "I'm sure we have met. Don't you remember? Where was it?"

I said, "Let's not worry about where we met before. It could drive us crazy trying to figure it out. I'll just say, it's great to see you again, and we'll leave it at that."

He agreed, but shook his head as he moved on to the next conversation.

A few minutes later, the other minister came out of the house, and when he came up to me, the same thing happened.

He also agreed to say, "It's great to see you again," and he moved on to the next conversation.

Larry looked at me and said, "What's that about?"

I haven't mentioned it before in this book, but this phenomenon has happened to me my whole life long. It still happens. Every time I encounter a member of the clergy, they always think they know me.

Strange, isn't it?

I can't even count the number of times it has happened to me. In the beginning, I thought it was funny, and I wondered why it kept happening.

By the time I was at Ted's grandmother's funeral, I had gotten used to it, and had stopped worrying about it. When I saw a clergyman approaching, I knew what was about to ensue, and I always reacted by saying what I had said to the ministers at this party.

I turned the question back to Larry and said, "Why do you think that happens to me?"

Larry hypothesized that, in a past life, perhaps I was one of the apostles, or someone in the direct circle of their God, Jesus.

"It's the only thing that makes any sense," he said. "Why else would they feel that they know you so well? Or perhaps you were Jesus. That would be pretty cool. Maybe I am hanging out with the reincarnation of Jesus right now."

I smiled at him wryly. I had certainly never considered anything like that before.

At this point of my life, I was in a position to be able to think about it seriously, though. All the time I had spent with John and all the things I had seen at least opened me up to the possibility of extraordinary things being true.

I have always felt a strong and unexplainable connection to Jesus.

Ever since I was a kid, any time I was laid open to the story of Jesus being hung on the cross—even if I saw it in a movie—I was wrecked. I experienced a myriad of deep emotions and energetic pain I could not explain, especially since I considered myself spiritual, not religious.

What do I actually feel about Jesus?

I feel intimately connected to Jesus and to his message. I believe he was a powerful teacher. I find it significant that Jesus never actually claimed to be God himself. He said we were all made in the image and likeness of God. He said that we could do anything and everything He did if we had faith to the same degree that He did. His message was a message of love, forgiveness, healing, and of light. I feel like I understand Him.

I think of the Bible as a book of metaphors and stories to bring us to a place of faith; it is not a documentary film. Stories change as they are told and handed down, and it is likely that this has happened to the writings in the Bible.

However, it is not for me to dictate other people's beliefs. You may have an entirely different view, and I do not question the validity of your beliefs. When it comes to organized religion, I agree to disagree, and I am okay with that. I have my own relationship with God, and it works for me.

Curb and Bakery Painting

When sales were down, Larry was the first of us to be fired from the car lot, and I was fired shortly after him. Neither one of us was making our minimum sales quota. It was not a job I was attached to—the only reason I had taken the job in the first place was because I knew, if I could survive that position, I could do anything.

At this point, I knew I wanted to continue to spend time with Larry, and he felt the same. However, we also needed to eat.

We received our last checks and wondered: *What we could do together to create income?*

As we sat on a curb in Larry's neighborhood contemplating our next move, Larry noticed that one driveway had their address number painted on the curb, but the one right next to it did not.

He said, "Keith, you know, everyone should have their address painted on their curb. How better for an emergency vehicle to see their address easily? That's something we can do. We can offer to paint the address on people's curbs for them. Rather than asking for a set price, we can ask them to give us what they feel it's worth to them. I think it's important, don't you? If they don't have any money, we will do it anyway. It will be like a public service."

"Great idea, let's do it."

"Between the two of us, we should have enough money for spray paint and number stencils. We should practice one or two times—let's do a few for free."

"Now you're thinking," I said. "This will be fun. It's a way for us to hang out and make money."

We went to the hardware store and got our supplies. We went to the first house and offered to do it free. We told them it was our first and wanted to know if it was okay if we practiced on their curb. They agreed. The number—black on a white square—came out clearly. The owner of the house saw our work, told us that it looked good, and handed us five dollars.

We went from house to house painting curbs. Some people refused, even when it was free. We remained unattached to the outcome. We were having fun being of service and making money while doing it. At the end of the day, we split the money we had made. It wasn't enough to pay rent, but it was enough to get a good meal and put a few groceries in the refrigerator. We did this for at least a month before the novelty and fun started to wear off. We were not making enough money painting curbs to pay the bills, so we asked God to show us what our next step should be.

At the end of our shift one day, we took our money and went to a local bakery to get a treat. At the bakery, we noticed the paint job inside was worn and fading.

I looked at Larry and said, "How much you think they would pay us to paint this?"

Larry said he didn't know.

He asked, "Have you ever painted a business interior? I haven't."

I had. I used to paint with my uncle. We painted exteriors and interiors of houses. Later, I worked for someone who did refurbishing of houses, which included everything and anything you can do inside of a house.

Larry started planning, "Okay. What is your idea of how we should paint it? We need to have something to tell them when we make an offer."

"What if we put a stripe that runs up the wall about four feet up, then goes up diagonally about three feet, and then goes the rest of the way parallel to the floor? In other words, two different colors divided by a white stripe. We will only have to get three colors of paint. The white will last a long time because we only use it for the stripe."

He liked where I was going with this so we sat down and considered the logistics.

How many gallons of paint would we need?

How much time would it take?

How much should we charge?

What would we do about customers being around all day?

We finished our treats and by then, we had agreed to the answers of these questions.

We went to the hardware store and priced paint, paintbrushes, tarps, rollers, and other supplies. We knew we would have to get half our salary up front to pay for the supplies. We crunched the numbers, and since I was the one with the most knowledge of painting, we decided that I would handle the quote.

We went back to the bakery, stepped up to the counter, and asked to speak with the owner.

He came out a few minutes later and asked, "How may help you?"

"We noticed that the paint job inside your store is old and fading. It sure would brighten this place up if you had a shiny new paint job."

"What did you have in mind?"

I explained my vision.

"Yes, I see it. That's very interesting. I don't have a lot of money. What were you thinking in the way of price?"

We gave him our price at four hundred dollars. We told him we'd start work as soon as he closed, and it would be painted and partially dry by the time he came in to open in the morning. We'd work through the night to get it done.

The owner stood there for about a minute, looking at the walls and the ceiling, and then said, "Will you do it for three hundred fifty dollars? If you will, we have a deal. And, just so you know, all the bakeries in this town, and in a few surrounding towns, belong to my family. You do a good job on this, and I'm sure others will consider hiring you as well."

I added, "And if they like the design, we can do the same in each building but with different colors. They can pick the two colors, and we will divide it with a white stripe like yours."

"That's a great idea. Do we have a deal?"

Larry and I had already discussed the lowest price we were willing to take, and this was fine. I shook his hand and we had a deal.

Staying up all night painting was tough. There were several other challenges and it was a learning experience. Fortunately, the job came out well, and we were hired by a second bakery at four hundred dollars. Ultimately, we painted five local bakeries with that custom design. It was a lot of work, but it was fun. And the rent was paid.

Vision in a Coffee Cup

I met Larry for breakfast one foggy Sunday morning. It was incredibly early, and I had been up for a couple of days straight, from doing crystal meth. I was still in my deep dark drug phase while working with John. Luckily, John didn't judge me for what I was doing. Sometimes, he actually partied right along with me. The funny thing was, no matter how much we partied, it never seemed to faze him in any way.

Larry and I were sipping coffee, catching each other up, and trying to decide what we would do that day. As he was sipping his coffee, he stopped and stared into the cup. He sat there mesmerized for what seemed like a few minutes. I didn't interrupt his process. I just sat there staring at him wondering what the hell was going on in that mind of his.

After a while, he looked up and said, "I gotta go."

"Where are you going?"

"Do you have time? Can you come with me? I had a vision. I saw it in my coffee cup. There was a winding mountain road, a great big tree, a sign with an arrow, and a church made of hay bales. There was a man who looked like a hermit. I don't know why, but I'm supposed to go to him. Are you coming?"

"Sure, I have nothing better to do today. I've been up for a few days. Don't mind me if I fall asleep."

"No problem. Sleep as much as you want. I'll drive."

As we drove out of town and headed towards the mountains, I dozed off. When I woke up, we were driving on a winding road that went up into the mountains. It wasn't long before we saw a remarkably large and beautiful tree.

Larry pointed to it and said, "That's the tree I saw in my coffee cup."

"Yeah. It's beautiful."

"Next thing to look out for is a sign that says *CHURCH* with an arrow pointing left."

"Okay, I will keep an eye out for it."

We drove for another half hour up the mountain before we both spotted the sign on the right-hand side of the road. We took a hard left and headed up a small mountain road. We followed the road for quite a while, and it ended at a farm. There was a huge grassy area with cars parked on it, and another sign that said *CHURCH,* with an arrow pointing to the right. We parked the car and headed to the barn. We assumed that the church service was inside the barn, and it seemed like we were right on time.

We entered the barn. Everyone was sitting on hay bales, facing a pulpit in the center of the barn. We took a seat in the back of the room. As soon as we sat down, the preacher stepped up to the pulpit and started the service. Larry scanned the room.

"The man I saw in my vision is over there, on the left. Do you see him?"

"Yeah, the scruffy looking guy with the long hair and hat on?"

"Yep, that's him all right. That's the man we were sent here to see."

"Do we wait until the end of the service or go and talk to him now?"

"Let's wait until the end of the service."

As soon as we stopped talking, the man looked over his shoulder at the two of us and waved as if he knew us or had been expecting us. The service was interesting, kind of a hard-core Christian revival. I thought it was a little funny, but then again, since I had been up for days, everything seemed a little funny. I was wishing I could take a nap and meet them outside, but I stayed at the service anyway. I didn't want to leave Larry alone.

After the service, the man walked over to us and said, "Welcome to my church. What did you think?"

Larry replied, "Now, that was quite a service. To God be the glory."

I said, "Not my cup of tea, but I'm here, aren't I?"

Ironic, given that it was a cup of coffee that brought us here.

The man smirked and said, "Somebody is ready for a nap."

I thought: *He read me pretty fast.*

We all walked outside of the barn towards Larry's car.

The old man said, "My name is Jim. I saw you in a vision I had this morning. I'm supposed to show you something. Will you drive me to my house?"

Larry answered, "Sure."

We all got in the car. I jumped into the back seat so Larry and Jim could be in the front and talk. We went down to the main road and took a left heading up the mountain. After a few miles, we took another left onto a small dirt road, and when the road ended, we pulled up next to a tiny camper. It was a camper designed to sit in the bed of a truck. Only there was no truck, just the camper, sitting on the ground.

The old man said, "Welcome to my home. Follow me."

I thought to myself: *Home? That's not a home, it's a glorified shack. How the hell are we all going to fit inside?*

We stepped inside and to the rear, where there was a picnic style table with benches underneath it. The old man offered us a cup of coffee.

I said, "Oh, yes, *please*."

I was so tired my face was about to hit the table. Even with the coffee, I soon had my head buried in my folded arms on the tabletop as Jim and Larry talked.

Jim told us how he had always been an old hippie type. He hated the consumer-driven culture. For a long time, he didn't know what he was going do with his life. Frustrated, he was about to give up when he received a call. His father had passed away. They had never been close, and he didn't actually know his father very well, but he went to the funeral. At the funeral, a lawyer asked if Jim would come see him the following day. Jim showed up to find that his father's will was being read. He was surprised he was asked to be there; since he didn't really know his father, he didn't expect to inherit anything.

Jim was wrong.

In the will, his father had written:

> *To my son, Jim:*
>
> *I leave you fifty acres of land in the San Joaquin Mountains. I hope you can do something with this land. It is beautiful and lush, but I never had any idea what to do with it except to*

hold onto it. When it came time to write this will, I realized I must have been holding onto it all this time so that I could give it to you. I know that if anyone can benefit from having this beautiful land, it will be you, son. I'm sorry I was never really there for you. I wish you all the best.

Love, Dad.

Jim concluded his story by saying, "So I took my last paycheck, bought this camper, and stuck it here, on my fifty acres of land. I've been here ever since, and I love it. This is sacred land. God has been good to me. He always provides what I need. I have little, and yet I have so much. I'd like to show you some of what I mean. Would you like to see?"

Of course, we did. I was exhausted, but I couldn't pass this up. I stood up, with effort.

Jim grinned at me and said, "Follow me. Keith, I think you will like this."

We started hiking. At one point, I was so tired that I could barely stand up. Jim encouraged me to hang in. He said there was a reward at the bottom of the trail. After a while, I thought I could hear water and asked about it.

The old man replied, "That's not just water, Keith, it's a magical spring. It's been blessed by God and has incredible restorative powers. Drinking from the spring is like drinking liquid electricity. It will heal whatever ails you."

I thought to myself: *Liquid electricity? What the hell is he talking about?*

At the bottom of the mountain was this beautiful spring. It looked like something that should be on a postcard. Perfectly lit, gorgeous trees, mini waterfall—everything I loved most about nature.

The old man said, "Take a drink, brother."

I reached down, scooped up some water in my hands, and drank it.

It's hard to explain what happened next using any words other than the ones the old man had already used.

It was, indeed, like drinking liquid electricity.

Each sip woke me up a little bit more and filled me up with more energy. The water made me feel as though I had just woken up from a lifetime of sleeping. I kept drinking from this magic spring. It felt like the first water I ever drank and the last I'd ever have. It made me feel wonderful. By the time I finished drinking, I was wide awake, and ready to go.

I thanked Jim. Whatever else Jim wanted to do now—I was definitely game.

Larry drank from the spring as well. He smiled at me with each gulp, looking at me with those incredible blue eyes as if to say: *I see what you mean.*

The old man took a few drinks himself, and then we headed back up the mountain. He showed us every site there was to see in this corner of his fifty acres. By the time we were back at the camper, I was still awake and feeling great.

He and Larry were swapping God and Jesus stories, speaking about journeys they had made. They talked about religion, discussed Bible passages, and caught up on many years of worship and study. Mostly, I sat back and listened, as I was not exactly a Bible scholar.

At some point in the conversation, Larry told Jim, "Keith has been working with an earthbound angel, who has been assigned to take him from not believing in anything to believing that everything is possible. He's been showing Keith miracle after miracle and has supported Keith in creating a few miracles himself. Keith is finally starting to believe, and he's been sent on a few journeys, like the funeral I told you about."

"So, you're a believer, Keith?"

"Yes, I guess I would say that I am," I replied. "I don't feel the need to go to church every week, I don't put my face in a book or anything, but my friend says that anything I can imagine is possible. Anything and everything is possible. He's taught me that words create—that what we say comes true."

I spilled out my life. I told him about my amazing experiences with John, the things I believed, saw, and experienced as a child, and the lesson about learning more by listening than by talking.

"That's pretty heavy," replied the old man. "So basically, this earthbound angel is teaching you to believe?"

"I think he is here to teach me all he can about life, creation, purpose, responsibility, and whatever else he can get into this tiny brain of mine. He's the most patient person I've ever met in my life. I have a thick skull. He's had to show me over, and over again. Somehow, he's done this without yelling at me even once. He says that someday, he will save my life, and once he does that he must leave, and go save someone else. I don't know what to make of it all. I just keep doing what I'm told to do and learning what I can."

Jim nodded.

I continued, "Being here today has taught me a lot. I mean, Larry saw you in a coffee cup, and here we are. I guess today is about all of us discovering why the two of you saw each other in a vision. That's what I'm interested in knowing."

The old man said, "The purpose of our meeting today will be revealed eventually. Today we're just supposed to connect, talk, laugh, enjoy each other's company, and trust that God will reveal why we met. The worst-case scenario is that I end up with two new good friends."

He looked at me and said, "I've already learned a few things from what you said and what Larry discussed regarding Bible interpretation. I've never heard things expressed the way he does. My mind is opening just by being around the two of you. It's not very often that I get company. Most people think I'm old, weird, and smelly."

The old man grinned at us, then he continued talking, "People are quick to judge, so very few take the time to ask me my name, let alone come up the mountain to my home and have a cup of coffee. The two of you have done more than most ever would. Few people have drunk from Magic Spring. I don't know how many years it's been since somebody sat down with me and spilled his heart out like you just did. It's been a long time since anybody trusted me with something so personal and sacred. You've done so much, and you sit there wondering what more there is for us to learn from each other."

We swapped stories for hours. Jim eventually opened up a few cans of beans and put them on the fire. We ate beans and bread, and something so simple felt like a feast fit for kings. Larry and I knew this man didn't have very much, but what he had he freely shared with us.

Two bits of information stand out when I think back on this old man:

- He had so little, but he was so happy.
- He had barely enough to survive, but he shared with us.

I came to understand that happiness is a decision. It is a way of being, and has absolutely nothing to do with money, stature, or toys. This man was truly happy, and I was so happy to have met him.

By the time we finished dinner, it was dark outside, and the conversation had turned to supernatural incidents. We talked about these in the same way as any other topic, which is unusual in itself.

Have you ever had something mystical happen to you?

If so, you understand that it's hard to talk about these happenings with most people—you know they will be doubtful or scared.

Anything to do with the supernatural is frightening for most people. In movies, the kinds of things I had seen and heard would be portrayed either as horror sequences, or as silly melodrama. Angels are usually seen as a kind of religious fantasy. Most people aren't receptive to conversing about the supernatural. Even if you have a friend who is accepting enough to listen, it is hard for someone to understand such experiences if they haven't lived through anything similar.

There's a kind of loneliness, as you can imagine, that comes from not being able to share your thoughts and experiences fully with the people closest to you. Perhaps you, also, have felt this way.

But on this night, I was able to be with two who understood the supernatural. Jim, Larry, and I freely shared our experiences with each other that night, and it felt wonderful to talk, and be truly understood.

Later in the evening, Jim asked us, "You want to see something really cool? Are you willing to open your mind to all possibilities?"

Larry and I agreed and went outside with Jim. He took us to the middle of the field of grass just north of his camper. We stood in a triangle and joined hands as Jim started to pray. I don't remember the exact words, but it went something like this.

> *Lord God we are so grateful for this day. I thank you so much for bringing my friends, Keith and Larry, to me. It has been a pleasure to meet them and to share wonderful stories. God, I believe they're open to seeing our friends. I believe it is part of the next steps in their evolution to see what you have shown me. Lord God, it is time for them to see the light. It's time for them to meet our friends. I ask you to share with my friends,*

> *show them! Lord God, show them, my dear friends, show up for them—show them the light!*

His voice got louder as he spoke. My eyes were closed as I focused on his words, believing in him, being willing to see what he was trying to evoke. The next thing we saw is hard to put into words.

Jim continued to repeat:

> *Lord God, show them, my dear friends, show up for them, show them the light…*

As he spoke, I heard a low tone buzzing loudly and becoming louder. Then, a bright light turned on. It startled me into opening my eyes. I looked across at Larry and Jim, and their hair was blowing. The low tone was still buzzing, and we were surrounded by a bright, intensely white light. I looked up, and there appeared to be some sort of craft or spaceship hovering above us; the buzzing came from there. I stared straight up in complete shock.

Jim's face was turned upward, with a wide smile.

He continued to speak:

> *Thank you, God, for showing them. Thank you, friends, for coming to visit us. Thank you—thank you—thank you!*

We were still holding each other's hands. Larry's eyes were bouncing from Jim, to me, to the light, to Jim, to me, to the light, and he was grinning from ear to ear. I'm sure the light was only on for a few minutes, but it seemed like an eternity.

I flashed back to my youth, when I was at a Boy Scout camp. I remembered lying on the ground, looking up at the stars, and seeing a few things in the sky that didn't appear to be stars. They were zigzagging, but not like planes or shooting stars.

I remembered thinking: *There is no way we are the only ones—there must be others out there somewhere.*

This flash of memory was in my mind when the beam of light turned off, and the low buzzing sound stopped. The three of us were still holding hands. We looked at each other and burst into spontaneous laughter.

Larry, still chuckling, looked at me, and said, "Was that cool—or what?"

I said, "Hell, yeah it was!"

The old man grinned at me, and then started to pray again:

> *Lord God, I want to thank you. Thank you for bringing me these two wonderful friends. Thank you for all that you've given me, for all the blessings, for the love, for all the joy, for this beautiful land, for the clothes on my back—dirty as they may be—for the beans and bread that we ate for dinner, for the church at the barn. Thank you, God, for everything. I am just so grateful to be alive. I'm so grateful to be here. I'm grateful that you were willing to show my new friends my connection with my alien friends. I'm grateful that I'm not the only one to see them. It makes me feel normal. I don't have to feel crazy anymore, as if I'm imagining stuff. God, I believe in everything, but seeing all that I've seen all by myself is not as great as sharing it with someone else. Thank you for the miracle. I'm so grateful, and all of this I say in the name of your son Jesus Christ, amen.*

Larry and I both answered, "Amen."

The three of us went back to Jim's camper, decompressed, savored our experience, and continued to share stories.

Just after one o'clock, Larry looked at me and said, "You ready to go?"

This day, which had started so simply, had become one that was filled with joys and wonders I could never have imagined. I would never forget it.

But he was right; it was time to leave.

6

Off of Drugs

During this time, my drug addiction was gradually stripping away my health, physically and emotionally. Soon, the deterioration started to accelerate, for both Rebecca and me. I hit my lowest low during this period when I slept only eight hours in thirteen days.

Live or Die: Make Your Choice

I hadn't seen John for some time, and I didn't know why. The time I was spending with Larry was picking up where John had left off as far as lessons and learning, but I missed John and wondered why he had disappeared.

I wasn't working at the bar anymore. When I went there to find John, he wasn't around. It was as if he had vanished. I was broke, strung out, and long overdue for some sleep when John finally showed up. At the time, I was on the couch in the living room with some other strung-out people. I was just sitting there, feeling sorry for myself, when I heard his truck pull up.

There was a knock at the door.

I opened it and said, "John, where have you been, man? I missed you so much."

He said nothing, came through the doorway, grabbed me by the arm, took me into the bathroom, and pointed at the mirror.

He said. "Look at yourself."

I said nothing as I looked at my tired body in the mirror.

He pointed again, and said, "At the rate you're going, you'll be dead in two weeks. You are at a choice point right now, and you need to choose. Live or die; make the choice."

I noticed the dark black rings under my eyes. I looked fifty years old, but I was only twenty-three.

Again, he asked for my choice, "What's it going to be—live or die? Make your choice."

He continued, "If I didn't love you, I'd be out there with those people in the living room, watching you slowly die. You need to make a choice, but, either way, I'm not sticking around to see it."

He disappeared as quickly as he came, and I was left standing in front of the mirror, alone. This man had the gift of sight. He had proven he could see things before they happened. I knew I had to answer his question.

Did I want to live?

I felt messed up and more depressed than ever. The next morning, I went out walking by myself to sort it all out. I knew I was out of control, but I didn't know what to do. I thought doing cocaine might relieve me of my misery. I stopped by my dealer's house to see if he would front me some drugs.

He said, "Yeah, I can't do that—and man, I think you need to go home right now and talk to your girl."

"Why? What do you know?"

"You just need to go talk to her now."

"Dude, you're freaking me out. Why are you saying this to me? What do you know?"

"She came by here a few hours ago, and she gave me this ring for some drugs."

He held up her engagement ring. She had taken our token of love and commitment and hawked it for drugs.

"She was talking crazy. She said she didn't need it any more, that she was going to kill herself with the eight-ball I gave her for the ring. I'm sorry, dude. I'm a drug dealer, not a marriage counselor."

I raced home expecting to find her dead with a needle hanging out of her arm. Instead, I came home to a blubbering mess of a woman. The drugs had made her sick, but didn't kill her. She blamed herself—and then she blamed me—for the situation we were in.

I felt betrayed. I felt as though the love I had for her was over. My typical piss-poor way of communicating kicked in, and I let loose with every hurtful thing I had been holding onto. I slammed the door on my way out.

I took off running up the street, crying and talking to myself. I had lost my job, my mentor and teacher, and now, my fiancé.

What did I have to look forward to anymore?

I remembered what John had said: *Live or die; make your choice.*

It occurred to me, suddenly, that I didn't really want to live. That thought slowed me down to a walk. I walked until I found myself standing on a freeway overpass watching the cars speeding underneath.

I thought: *It could all be over if I just jumped and was hit by one of those cars.*

I started to climb up over the rail.

I had one leg over the fence, when I heard a man's voice say, "Hey! What are you doing?"

He grabbed me and pulled me back.

I said, "What do you think I'm doing? Just leave me alone."

He said, "I remember you. You're the bartender from Silver Dollar Hofbrau. You were one of the happiest people I'd ever met. What the hell happened?"

I asked him again to leave me alone.

He said, "I'll make you a deal. If you let me take you to the Silver Dollar and buy you a drink, I'll listen to your story. If I can't convince you that life is worth living by the end of our conversation, I will let you go right back to the freeway overpass."

I agreed. I thought I could ditch him at the Silver Dollar, and get it done before he could grab me again.

We sat at one of the tables and talked. I don't remember the details of the conversation we had, but I do remember telling him about the last six months of my life. I told him how my friend had stood me in front of the mirror and told me that, at the rate I was going, I would be dead in two weeks.

He leaned forward and said, "If God sends you two people in two days to save your life, maybe you should listen. You are at a choice point here. Live or die, make your choice."

I excused myself to go to the rest room. Something was nagging me. I knew there was something I should be paying attention to, but it was eluding me. I went over our conversation in my mind.

When I got to the part where he said: *You are at a choice point here. Live or die, make your choice*, I realized that was exactly what John had said the day before, word for word.

When I came out of the bathroom to ask the man about what he said, he was gone. I stood there, feeling dazed and confused.

Could it have been John trying to save me again, but this time appearing to me in another form?

I walked out of the bar. To my left was the freeway overpass; to my right was my walk home.

I took a breath and heard the words again: *You are at a choice point here. Live or die, make your choice.*

By now, those words were ringing—echoing in my head.

Live or die, make your choice.

Live or die, make your choice.

I decided to walk home.

As I walked, I tried to sort through everything that had happened. I couldn't deny that two people in two days had tried to save my life.

Had God really sent them?

Did this mean that I should choose to live?

Then, another thought occurred to me: *Had God sent the same person in two different forms to save my life?*

My training with John enabled me to believe that this was a possibility, but wasn't it a spectacular amount of effort to spend on one person?

I wasn't worth the effort: That's what I was really thinking.

Believing I wasn't worthwhile was keeping me from seeing what was right in front of me. Finally, I started to entertain the possibility that maybe someone else thought I was worth the effort. In any case, it was clear to me that someone or something was trying desperately to save my life. There must be some reason why.

I must be here for a reason.

By the time, I reached the apartment I had chosen life.

When I shared this story with Rebecca, and told her I was quitting the drugs, she decided she would quit along with me. We knew we needed to move out of that drug-dealing apartment or we would never make it. Initially, we found another apartment in Fresno, but the town was a constant reminder of my drug-induced past. We decided to move back to our hometown.

We packed up our station wagon and were about to drive off, when I heard a familiar-sounding truck. I looked off in the distance and saw John driving our way.

He pulled up, got out of the truck, walked up to me, and held out his hand.

He said, "Give it to me."

I looked at him with a puzzled look on my face. He pointed to Mel's ring on my finger.

Do you remember the last time he asked for my ring?

It was right after we had started to get to know each other. Holding the ring, he had told me all about my past, and my future.

I took off the ring and put it in his palm. He closed his hands around it and closed his eyes. He was doing what is called a *life review*. Those with the gift of site can take an object that has someone's energy in it, hold it, and see a life from beginning to end.

I waited and watched him.

Finally, he smiled, opened his eyes, handed me back the ring, and said, "Congratulations. You live to be a very old man."

I started to weep. I thanked him for everything he had done for me.

He smiled and said, "You're welcome, young man. Now go, start fresh. Be the difference maker you were born to be."

I hugged him, wiped away my tears, and left. I knew I needed to go, but driving away from John was one of the hardest things I've ever done in my life.

What the Future Would Bring

I chose life.

I cleaned up and moved back to my hometown with Rebecca.

Years later, when I was missing John and thinking about when we met, I remembered what the first words out of his mouth were.

Do you remember?

"He'll learn."

Then, I remembered the story he told me about the boy who forgot to be a boy, the boy who had a strong bond with a guardian angel, the one who had grown up and shunned his great powers.

Do you remember this first conversation?

> *…this boy was visited by a guardian angel when he was in his twenties, and the angel took him to do things he never got to do as a child. He showed the boy miracles beyond human belief. The angel saved that boy's life and restored his faith. Once the boy, now a man, was on the right path, the angel left to save another soul…*

As I was thinking about him, I had a revelation that hit me like a ton of bricks:

John was another guardian angel, but this time, in the flesh.

He came into my life, did all he said he would do, saved my life, and then he was gone, just as he had foretold.

At that moment, I could hear his voice, and his laugh, and I remembered all the conversations I had with my angel when I was a boy. I was amazed it had taken me so long to put it all together.

Was this my guardian angel from so long ago?

Had I lived a modern-day miracle?

With my mind wide open, I thought of other possibilities:

Was he also Larry?

Was he the man who had saved me from jumping over the freeway overpass fence?

Or were they all separate angels, all watching over me?

I couldn't be sure.

Part III

Turning My Back, Opening My Heart

7

Moving, the Car Accident, and the Arrival of My Son

The next period of my life was not as filled with angels as the last, and I know it was partially my own doing. I refer to this time as a *spiritual drought*. I experienced fewer angel communications than any other period. However, it did have its share of miracles and wondrous guidance.

It was an important part of my journey because of what I learned, the books I read, and, most especially, the people I met. Additionally, it was a time to tune into my inner guidance system and to learn to trust my inner knowing.

When Rebecca and I arrived back in our hometown, we went to my mother's house. She offered to put us up until we could find a place to live.

The first night we were there, I connected with a friend I hadn't seen for six years. It was fun going down memory lane and catching up, until he reached down and grabbed a mirror that had crystal meth on it. He chopped it up and made three lines. He snorted the first line and passed it to me.

Without a thought, I quickly snorted my line and handed it to Rebecca, who followed suit.

I know, I know—you're thinking: *What are you doing, Keith!?*

I was thinking the same thing.

I tried to stay focused on what my friend was saying, but all I could think about was the huge mistake I had just made. I told him I had to go, grabbed Rebecca, and we took off.

We drove around for hours, both of us crying, trying to process what we had done. We thought about our time with John and all that had transpired to save my life. We pulled up to my mother's place to sleep on the floor of her living room, laid there in silence and stared at the ceiling all night, tweaking on speed, with nothing but our thoughts and our guilt. This was the last time that either one of us put anything white up our noses.

My recovery was off to a bad start. I was intensely disappointed with myself. I felt like I had already let God down—as well as my guardian angel, Rebecca, and myself. After this lapse, I was even more determined to persevere.

In retrospect, I probably should have taken my journey to recovery alone, but I was still holding onto the hope that my relationship with Rebecca was heaven sent and would last. We both still wanted to make it work.

The next day, we reached out to Rebecca's aunt and uncle, who owned a number of apartment buildings in our town. We went to their house, told them our situation and, before we left, we had jobs as apartment managers for their biggest building. We were paid in free rent, phone, and electricity. We could elect to do any jobs the building needed for additional pay—jobs that might otherwise be farmed out. When someone moved out of the building, for example, we could do the painting and carpet cleaning. This extra money helped as I looked for another job.

The Car Accident

Eventually, Rebecca and I got corporate jobs for the same company, but at different buildings. I would drop her off and pick her up after work.

Although I wasn't generally a speeder, Rebecca had a habit of checking my speed. One night, when we were driving home, she asked me how fast I was going.

I replied, "I'm doing twenty-eight and the speed limit is thirty."

No sooner had I answered than I looked to my left and saw a car speeding directly toward us from a side street. The car smashed into us just behind my door, and our car slid sideways. Everything moved into slow motion as the car flipped through the air. The world turned in our front car window. I was holding on for dear life, since I did not have my seatbelt fastened.

As one hand came off the wheel, at the top of my lungs, I yelled, "No!"

In that moment, I felt my angels holding me in place. The car continued flipping and spinning and eventually, landed upside down. When it came to a stop, I was sitting with my legs crossed on the ceiling of the overturned car.

To my right, I could see Rebecca hanging upside down. She had been wearing her seatbelt, and it was tethering her to the seat.

I couldn't believe I was still in the car. I should have been tossed from the vehicle. Rebecca asked me for help; the seatbelt that was holding her in place was hurting her. I reached up and freed her. She landed hard, and we both crawled out.

Still in shock, I immediately took off toward the car that hit us. I was looking for the driver so I could give him a piece of my mind.

I found myself yelling, "You could have killed us!"

The accident had happened in front of a house where a party was going on, and several people were in the front yard right next to where our car landed. I was intercepted by one of them, who helped me calm down.

He said, "Dude, you need to relax. Your head is bleeding. The police will deal with that guy when they get here."

He took me back to Rebecca and instructed us to sit down. He told us that he had seen the whole incident, and the police had already been called.

The windshield glass had broken, and Rebecca and I both had cuts from the glass. Blood was running down our faces. Soon, the police arrived and attempted to sort it all out. Shortly after their arrival, the ambulance came, and we were sped off to the hospital.

It was my first time in an ambulance with the siren on. As I lay strapped to the gurney, I looked up and saw a handful of angels hovering over me.

I said to them, "Thank you for saving me."

They nodded, smiled, and then disappeared from my sight. I was so grateful to know they were still with me, and it was a joy to see them again. The mistake I had made with the drugs was fresh in my mind, and I had been feeling thoroughly ashamed of myself. I was so relieved to see that my angels hadn't abandoned me. I closed my eyes and tried to relax for the rest of the ride to the hospital.

Rebecca and I were taken to the ER. It was remarkable that we were alive to tell the story of what had happened. We both had whiplash and multiple contusions from the shattered windshield. Rebecca's ribs were severely bruised from hanging upside down. I ended up having some issues with my neck for years afterward. But we were alive, and that is what mattered.

When the responding officer arrived at the hospital to get our account of what had happened, he told us that the other driver was at fault. He said the eyewitnesses agreed that the driver was going somewhere between forty and fifty miles per hour, and didn't even attempt to stop at the stop sign he had passed before hitting us. There were no tire skid marks—he hadn't even tried to stop before hitting us. The passengers of the other car were fine. We learned that our car had been totaled.

After the officer left, the doctor came in and told Rebecca and I the results of our tests. Again, I saw three angels hovering above us. I smiled as they listened to the doctor share his findings. After he was finished, they once again disappeared from sight.

Time for a Child

A few days after the accident, we went to get our belonging from the totaled car. One item that we never found was Rebecca's packet of birth control pills.

When we didn't find them, Rebecca said, "Maybe it's a sign. Maybe it's time."

Rebecca had been wanting to have a child, but I wasn't ready. It wasn't because I didn't want to be a father; it was because we were still having some critical relationship issues. Our communication was still as horrible as ever and, frankly, I wasn't sure we were going to make it together.

We had promised each other that, if we had a child, we would never divorce. So, for me, agreeing to have a child was committing to our relationship forever. I wasn't feeling too certain about forever.

We argued over this for months. Finally, she wore me down. I felt backed into a corner, and I agreed. To be honest, with all the drugs we had done over the years, I thought we would have little chance of conceiving anyway.

I was wrong. We were quite fertile after all. The first time Rebecca's period was due, it didn't come. After a week, she bought a pregnancy test, and it came back positive. I couldn't believe my eyes.

We set a date to get married. We decided to keep our marriage ceremony as simple as we could. As a wedding present, Rebecca's aunt and uncle gave us money to plan the wedding—thank God. Without their support, we would have gotten married by the justice of the peace down at the courthouse, and our future might have been more complicated. You'll see what I mean later in this chapter.

We arranged to have the ceremony under our favorite tree in a park across from the high school. We had both graduated from that school and had enjoyed picnics under that tree when we were young. It was the most romantic—and inexpensive—place that we could think of. My best man was a friend I'd had since junior high school, and Rebecca's bridesmaid was her sister. It was a nice ceremony with a reception immediately following. Rebecca arrived late, which freaked me out a bit, but at least she didn't leave me at the altar.

It's a Boy

After what seemed like years—not just forty weeks—of living with a woman who ate strange things, could turn to pure evil in five seconds, and then be laughing two minutes later, Rebecca's water broke.

I prayed for a quick and easy birth. What happened was quite the opposite.

We arrived at the hospital and got a bed. She was having contractions, but not often enough for the labor to progress much. Time ticked by so slowly. Rebecca had vowed she would give birth without drugs, but as time went on, her discomfort and pain started to overwhelm her. By the time the contractions were a few minutes apart, Rebecca had threatened to kill me, had told me this was all my fault, and had accused me of other horrible things.

After a while, we lost track of how long we'd been at the hospital.

Soon, Rebecca was at the end of her rope. I tried to calm her, but nothing I said helped.

She cried, "I know I agreed that I wouldn't use drugs, but I'm over that. It hurts. It hurts so much I can't take it anymore. I want the drugs."

In planning for the birth, we had agreed that it would be my job to talk her through the pain, so I said, "Honey, you can do this. I believe in you. Just remember to breathe."

She glared at me and said, "Look, Motherfucker, you did this to me. You fix it now. Get me drugs right now, or I will kill you where you stand."

I went out to find a nurse or doctor to tell them we had decided she would be taking the drugs.

The doctor and the nurse prepared to give her an epidural and suggested I leave during the process. I told Rebecca I would return after she was feeling better. She said that was fine, and I promptly ran out of the room.

I met her sister and a few other family members in the waiting room, and we went to the cafeteria. As I was telling them about our trials, from a place deep inside me, I suddenly heard Rebecca screaming.

I could hear her as clearly as if she were standing next to me. "Keith, I need you! Where are you, Keith?"

I dropped my fork, looked at Rebecca's sister, and said, "I have to go right now. She needs me."

I flew across the quad and up the hallway to the elevators. I felt as if I were running through water. When I entered the room, it was empty. The place was a wreck; it looked like a twister had come through the room.

I came back to the nurse station and asked, "Where is my wife? How is my wife?"

The nurse explained, "When the doctor went to administer the epidural, the baby's heart beat started to indicate stress, and they discovered that the umbilical cord was wrapped around the baby's neck. They took your wife in for an emergency cesarean birth. The good news is you have a baby boy, and he's healthy."

I looked at them and said, again, "Where is my wife? How is my wife?"

One nurse looked at the other and said, "Isn't that sweet? Usually, the father just wants to know how the baby is."

I glared at her and said, "If you don't answer my questions, we are going to have a real problem."

The nurse promptly took me to see my wife. She was doped up and barely awake when I entered the room.

She mumbled, "I was so scared. I called out to you, but you weren't there. There was a problem, so they brought me here and took the baby out. He's okay. I'm going to go to sleep now."

Rebecca faded off from pure exhaustion, and the nurse took me to see my son. He was so beautiful and, thankfully, strong and healthy.

Communication, Communication, Communication

Real life isn't like it is in the movies. Babies don't make things better for a relationship, and no handbook on parenting can tell you how to handle all the changes gracefully.

To say things were tough at home is an understatement. Our child, whom we named Timar, was healthy, and we had good jobs. Having a new baby, however, is a stressful time for any couple, and our poor communication skills didn't help. We were doing the best we could, but that wasn't particularly good.

Rebecca left her job and stayed home with the baby. I continued working my corporate job—in sales administration at a major multinational electronics company—and I hated it. The baby had colic, which meant none of us was getting much sleep. I agreed to take half of the night shifts with Timar. The only thing that would help the baby sleep was to put him in the car seat and drive around. Unfortunately, as soon I put him back in his crib, he would wake up screaming. Home life was a disaster. My job was a nightmare. Something, as they say, had to give.

What almost gave was my heart.

The stress of my corporate sales job began to affect my health, and seriously. One day, I was feeling so awful that I left work in the middle of the day to see a doctor. My blood pressure reading at the doctor's office was dangerously high. They checked my heart and the tests came back normal; my symptoms were all from the high blood pressure. On that day, it became clear to me that the stress from my job was killing me. I knew I had to leave this job, but I had Rebecca and the baby at home. Responsibilities came first.

On the way home from the doctor, I stopped at the retail store of an electronics chain, and I saw that they were hiring. Since I'd been working for nearly three years for a top electronics company, I gave it a shot. The manager liked my tenacity and hired me. I didn't need my old boss for a reference, and I didn't need two more weeks of stress. I went back to the office, quit, and picked up my last paycheck.

The electronics store was part of a chain. This was my first retail experience. Gus, the general manager of the store, took me under his wing. He had a way about him that put everybody at ease.

I started in the personal electronics section, where every new sales employee began. The most successful salesperson in the department was a man named Ken. Because of the competitive nature of sales, the other employees would talk about him, disparagingly, behind his back. This didn't make any sense to me. I decided to learn from him instead. He was visibly surprised when I asked for his help.

Collaboration and cooperation can be a very successful combination. Not only was I learning to be a great salesperson, but I also enjoyed hanging out with Ken. He was a great guy, and over time, he became a good friend of mine. Unfortunately, even though I was doing well as far as my sales numbers were concerned, there was nothing satisfying about the job, and it wasn't long before I was ready to change jobs.

I commented to another salesman one day that I needed to get out.

I said, "I don't care if a big screen TV falls on me. I need to get out."

I should have remembered my power to manifest. The next day I was asked to help with a delivery, which was something completely—and annoyingly—outside of my job description.

What do you think we were we delivering?

You guessed it—a big screen TV.

And what do you think happened next?

You guessed it. The TV fell on me.

At the ER, the doctor told me I had a pinched nerve in my neck and a polyp between the C6 and C7 vertebrae in my neck. He shared different options for treatment, gave me a prescription for pain pills, and sent me on my way. I headed into physical therapy, and then to a job placement company—since there was no way I was returning to that retail position.

At the job placement company, I was given a battery of tests. They showed that, for the basics you learn in school, I had a low aptitude—no surprise there—but for the more problem-oriented and engineering areas, I was a good fit. My counselor, Tim, gave me some educational programs to look at, and I chose to enroll in an audio/video engineering training program in Los Angeles. With Tim's help, I got in.

The program curriculum was like a dream come true. However, the commute, classes, and homework took nearly all my time, which annoyed Rebecca. She kept saying she wanted more support from me. I tried to explain that getting this degree would mean getting a job I could enjoy and that would pay well. Going this route, to me, *was* supporting her. She didn't see it that way.

Rebecca's resentment, to be sure, made this time of my life difficult for me. Still, I worked hard and had high marks through the first part of the semester, which was the audio part of the program. I enjoyed the audio section, but the video part of the coursework rekindled my love of movies and made me start thinking again about the childhood dream I'd had of being a director.

Crystal

About halfway through this section, the president of the training school called me into his office. My first thought was that something had happened to Rebecca or my son.

Instead, I heard that my half-sister, Crystal, had been murdered.

Her funeral was a few days from then. The president told me not to worry about school—he told me to go be with my family. I could return to the program whenever I was ready.

You will be wondering who Crystal is. Years after my mother and father divorced, my father had remarried. His new wife didn't have any children of her own and wasn't too fond of my sister and me.

Dad and his new wife adopted two children. First, a boy named David, followed a few years later by a girl named Crystal. For years, I felt like my stepmother had purposely conjured replacements for my sister and me, but I never held it against my new adopted brother and sister. They were both absolutely beautiful in their own way.

One summer, I spent a few weeks with my dad, stepmother, and David, when he was five years old. My stepmother made this trip a living hell for me, but the highlight was being with little David. He was so sweet and cute. The time we spent together was far too short, but it felt good to know I had a brother, even though we were clear across the country from each other. My father lived in Virginia, and I lived in California.

Long after they had adopted Crystal, I went to visit my father again. I was grown then. David was a young adult, and Crystal was a teenager. It was the first time I would meet Crystal in person. We'd spoken to each other a few times on the phone. Because my stepmother closely monitored all calls, we were never able to really connect.

When I met Crystal in person—I mean from the moment our eyes locked—it felt like we had known each other for lifetimes before.

It wasn't a meeting of uncomfortable silence, a handshake, and a *nice-to-meet-you.*

It was more like: *How have you been, beloved? How have you been since the last lifetime we were together?*

We hit the ground running and gained a lot of ground in very little time. My stepmother was still constantly monitoring the three of us. It was as if she wanted to make sure we had no time together to bond; or perhaps, to compare stories of the past.

One night, David, Crystal, and I all waited the parents out. My stepmother couldn't stay awake forever. Once she gave up and went to bed, we got together and really connected. There were some stories that Crystal had heard about me that didn't make any sense to her, and she wanted to know the truth. As I had expected, my stepmother had told them some things about me that were incomplete or downright false.

I told her my side of the stories she had heard, and she said, "Okay, now it all makes sense."

By the time I left this short visit with my Virginia family, I felt as close to Crystal as I did to my other sister, Tina. This is really saying something, because Tina had all but raised me. As I said before, it was as if I had known Crystal for a thousand years before. We had a few phone conversations after this trip. Then, at one point, she challenged my stepmother one too many times, and had to move to another family's home. We lost touch after that.

Now, I had just been told that Crystal had been murdered by her so-called boyfriend. She was in an abusive relationship and had told her boyfriend she couldn't take it anymore. She told him she was breaking up with him. He was not having that. The rest of the story is straight out of a horror movie—and certainly not one I would ever want to watch.

I made plans and flew to Virginia to be at her funeral service. At the funeral, I fell apart.

You know that character in the movies who falls down and weeps on top of the casket at a funeral?

Yep, that was me. I lost it, big time. This loss was a tough one for me. I was beating up on myself for not staying in touch. I felt like I had let her down, because I wasn't there to protect her from this fate.

During the week after returning home, I was still an emotional wreck. School was the one thing that was going well. I decided to return and try to graduate with my class. I had to work harder and longer hours than before, which made my home life even worse. I needed Rebecca's support, and she wasn't there for me in any way.

Graduation and a Difficult Decision

I persevered and graduated with perfect grades. This was an amazing feat for a guy who barely graduated high school, and had only done a year and a half of community college. I was proud of my accomplishments and looked forward to finding a job as an audio or video engineer.

When I came home from my graduation ceremony, my mother and sister, Tina, were waiting for me. My wife was visiting her sister for a few days, and she had my son with her. We celebrated my graduation, but I could tell something was wrong; Tina and my mother were acting funny. After some convincing, they told me that they had learned that Rebecca had cheated on me again.

The next several hours found me pacing the room, crying, and praying to God:

> *I don't know what to do here, God. You are the one who sent me a guardian angel to tell me that this woman was going to be my wife. I have done everything I can. I've gotten myself off drugs, gotten married, and had a child. I'm doing my best to provide for my family. Why is this happening?*
>
> *It's been a long time since I've heard my angels tell me what to do, a long time since you told me what to do. I'm feeling alone. If ever I needed you to give me a sign, now is that moment. Rebecca and I promised we would never divorce if we had a child. There's a lot riding on this decision. I don't know what to do. Lord, give me a sign, and make it obvious, make it clear.*

As soon as I finished this monologue, I heard a voice clearly over my shoulder tell me: *Go to the filing cabinet.*

I walked over to the filing cabinet.

Again, the voice spoke: *Open the filing cabinet.*

"Okay, now what?"

Flip through the files. There, stop there.

The file I had stopped on said *Marriage Certificate* on it.

Open the file and read.

I found a sealed stamped envelope, and it was addressed to the California County Recorder. I opened it and found our marriage certificate inside, signed by Rebecca, the preacher, our witness, and me. Our marriage certificate had never been mailed.

I thought to myself: *There could be no clearer sign than this.*

The next day I called my sister and asked her if she would do some research for me. I asked her to call the hall of records to check if there was any evidence of our marriage. She searched but there was none. I knew exactly what I needed to do.

When Rebecca returned from her sister's house with my son, I told her I had found out about her infidelity. I told her I was done trying to please her and that I wanted out. A divorce wasn't necessary since there was no legal record of our marriage.

She was in shock, of course.

"What about our son? He'll be living with me, right?"

I told her that didn't seem fair given her part in this, and she unexpectedly agreed.

We amicably split our belongings and checked with a lawyer about custody. He told us that, even though there was no marriage certificate filed, in California, we had been together long enough to qualify for common-law marriage. It wasn't hard to dissolve, but it had to be done legally. The good news was that common-law marriages were a lot easier when it came to paperwork and cost.

We were clear about how our property was to be divided.

When the time came to discuss custody, Rebecca said, "It's up to our son who he lives with once he gets old enough to make those types of decisions. For now, he will live with his father."

We filed the paperwork, and the divorce was final.

On the day before Thanksgiving, she moved out.

8

Overwhelming Loss and Blocking the Flow

The holidays were tough that year. I participated in the usual Thanksgiving rituals, but even spending time with my family did nothing to improve my mood. Christmas wasn't any better. As the New Year approached, I made a decision. The coming year was going to be completely different for me.

On January 2, I hit the ground running, looking for a job. At first, I was planning to become an audio engineer. I was a musician, after all, and I had long dreamed of being able to make my own album, so this seemed to be a good direction to choose. I found a listing of all the audio recording facilities in Hollywood and Burbank. I drove around to each place, offering to start at a decent wage. What I was offered in return was a pill that was hard to swallow.

The energy I was met with was the very opposite of inviting. I was so disappointed. Positions were scarce at the time, and it appeared that, if I wanted to work in the audio industry, I would have to start as an unpaid intern—and even those internship positions were hard to find.

I would have to shift gears.

Okay, then, video it is.

I found a book that listed all the video production houses in the area. They were listed in the book by the type of production.

I asked myself: *In a perfect world, what kind of job would I like to do in the video business?*

I had always wanted to be a film director, but I was pretty sure I couldn't show up to a film production house, say I want to be a director, and get hired on the spot.

I decided I would try the Foley houses first. A Foley artist is the person who makes the physical sounds that are put inside of a movie. I didn't get anywhere. I learned that this part of the industry was comprised of all family houses—you couldn't get in without a connection of some kind—so I couldn't even get a foot in the door. I turned to TV production companies, and, initially, didn't have any luck.

Frustrated, I put my manifesting powers to work.

I set my focus: *The next place I go to will be the last place I have to apply. I'm going to get a good job, and I'm going to get one right now.*

I drove a half mile down the road to the next TV production house on my list.

I was greeted by a woman who said, "Welcome to Face Broadcast Productions. I am Jamie, and I am one of the owners of this company. The other owner is the video engineer in that room you're looking into. Turn around and wave, Ron."

A man turned around and waved.

"That's my ex-husband. He owns this place with me."

The interview was more like a casual conversation, with both of us relaxed and laughing. She gave me a tour of their small facility.

When we got back to the reception area, Jamie said, "It was very nice to meet you. I'm going to talk with my partner at the end of the day, and I will call you tomorrow and let you know our decision."

The next day, early in the morning, the phone rang. I had the job.

I've worked for many different companies in my life, but working for Face Broadcast Productions was the best experience I ever had. It was a lot of work and a lot of hours—up to sixty hours per week at times—and I enjoyed every minute of it.

My sister was in an unhealthy relationship, and had been having a tough time with my nephew, so he came to live with us. The three of us—my son, my nephew, and I—moved to Glendale, California. I enjoyed my time with the two of them, but had a terrible case of *empty bed* syndrome. After nearly fourteen years together, it was strange not having Rebecca in the bed next to me each night. My son was struggling a bit in school, and he was missing his mother too.

Fortunately, shortly after I started working at Face Broadcast, my sister left the unhealthy relationship she'd been in, and came to live with us. She needed a place to stay, and since I was working so many hours a week, I welcomed the help with the boys.

I was even more grateful to have her around during the next period of my life.

To this day, I think of it as *the year when everyone died.*

I had already lost my little sister, Crystal. Then, within eight months, I lost two of my closest friends, Keni and Jeffrey, as well as my aunt, my grandmother, and another friend from high school, Steve.

One of my friends died from being so physically overweight that his heart couldn't take it anymore. One committed suicide. Another friend fell out of a moving vehicle and died. My aunt died of cancer, and my grandmother died of old age. She slowly slipped away, lost her memory, and passed in a full care facility at the age of eighty-seven.

Another Funeral

All the losses were terrible, but Jeffrey's death was harder for me because he had taken his own life. At his service, I learned that he had Lupus and had been in pain for years.

I had spoken with Jeffrey only a few months before. He had invited me over to his place saying he had something he wanted to talk to me about. I told him I could come over shortly with my wife and my son, but he said he needed me to come alone. I said I couldn't come unless they came with me, so he declined. That was the last time I spoke to him.

Why didn't you just go over and see him?

I was feeling so guilty.

What if I could have saved him from taking his life?

When I called my mother and told her Jeffrey was gone, she asked if she could join me at the funeral. After the service, we went to Jeffrey's parents' house where people were coming together to mourn his passing. In the backyard was a little house where my friends were hanging out.

As soon as I crossed the threshold into the little house, something came over me. Everything inside the house faded, and I saw Jeffrey stand up on a chair, slip a noose over his neck, and kick the chair out from under him. I watched him hang himself. I physically experienced it. After his body became lifeless, the picture faded out, and everyone inside of the room faded back in. I knew I was going to throw up, so I took off toward the bushes in the backyard.

I passed my mother in the yard on the way out.

She pointed back at the little house, and she said emphatically, "Don't go in there!"

I said, "Too late," and I threw up in the bushes.

Once I had finished, I wiped my mouth and sat down next to my mother. We compared notes, and I discovered that she had seen exactly what I had.

The Buddhists believe that the body of a corpse should not be touched in any way for three to eight hours after breathing ceases. They believe that the spirit of a person will linger on in the area for some time, and, during this time, others can be affected by what happened to the corpse. Perhaps his essence was still there, and we tapped into it.

Overwhelmed by Loss

All these deaths were too much for me to process. I had no experience with loss at this level. All of a sudden, so many of the people I loved had been taken from me.

Before this year, I could find the silver lining in every situation, but not this time. People around me would tell me they were sorry. They would ask me to let them know if they could do anything to support me, but I had no idea what to ask for.

Have you ever felt this way?

Sometimes, you want help, and you know that people are willing to offer help, but if you don't know *what* you need, how do you know what to ask for?

The best advice I can offer you is to let people in anyway—sometimes just by being there, a friend can give you exactly what you need in the moment. Shutting friends out is never a good solution to your problems.

Of course, I didn't take my own advice at this time.

At this point, I stopped talking and connecting with people. I would show up to work, do my job, and go home. I was crushed—broken—and my will to bring others good cheer was at an all-time low.

It was easy to slip into work mode and not pay attention to what was eating me up inside. Most people didn't notice the change in me. They were all too busy working toward deadlines. One producer, Donna-Lisa Valencia, was the exception. She realized I was hurting deeply and wanted to do something to get me to process these feelings instead of burying them. She knew that repressing my feelings was hurting me.

When Christmas came that year, Donna-Lisa gave me the greatest gift—a copy of the book, *Chicken Soup for the Soul: 101 Stories to Open the Heart and Rekindle the Spirit*. The book, by Jack Canfield and Mark Victor Hansen, had been out since 1993, but I had never heard of it.

Inside the cover, she had written:

> *Keith—*
>
> *For the most smilin' guy I know.*
>
> *I know this year's been hard, so here's a little something to help you keep the faith!*
>
> *Merry Christmas,*
>
> *Donna-Lisa.*

Tears came to my eyes as I felt her love and support.

Starting the next day, I would read the stories in the book each day at lunchtime. I was slowly coming back. Reading how other people dealt with tragedy was therapeutic for me. I was able to take comfort from the stories. At the same time, the book helped me to realize the senselessness of declining the support and assistance that my friends had been offering all along.

Once I was feeling better, I began to let people back in. I slowly started to feel good again. The experience of living through that year has helped me process my way through other losses. It has also allowed me to better support others through their losses.

Throwing the Walls Up and Blocking the Flow

My sister, Tina, and I had a special relationship. Since she is the one who raised me, I was closer to her than anybody in my life, other than my mother. Once my sister came to live with me as an adult, it was apparent just how close that connection was. One night we were watching TV and I had chosen a show that I liked.

I heard my sister say, "God, I hate this show, I wish you would just change the channel."

So, I picked up the remote control, changed the channel to something I knew she liked, and said, "Okay, there you go—are you happy now?"

She looked puzzled.

"What are you talking about?"

"You just said, 'God, I hate this show. I wish you would just change the channel.'"

"No, I didn't."

"Yes, yes, you did!"

"Okay, I did, but I didn't say it out loud. I said it inside my head. Are you kidding me? You're inside my head? I can't even have my own thoughts now, without you here in them?"

"Oh . . . I . . . I didn't know."

"This is insane, Keith. I'm not sure I can handle you in my head like that."

Sometimes knowing things before they happen, or hearing people's thoughts, is more of a curse than a gift. For years, I wondered why I could shake somebody's hands, look in their eyes, and know their life story to about 90 percent accuracy. I wondered why I knew things long before they happened, and how it was that sometimes I could hear what people were thinking.

When I was young, it was hard to make sense of this kind of knowledge, but John had opened me up to believe in my own possibilities. I now understood what was happening, but that didn't mean I liked it.

After I left John in Fresno and moved back to my hometown, I had mostly disconnected from my abilities. Once I started the TV production job, I started to tune in again, and the floodgates opened. Sometimes it was fun, but often it was challenging. It could be horrifying. Sometimes, it felt nothing like a gift.

Can you imagine knowing ahead of time that something terrible and tragic is going to happen?

Can you imagine how it feels to know, but have no way to stop it?

After this incident with my sister, something else happened that made me decide to put up a wall again.

At Face, we had hired a young woman named Gina. She enjoyed her work with the video company, but her goal was to be a professional model. We worked long hours together, and although I wasn't ready to date again, I fell for her. Nothing ever happened between us, although I did meet her family and visited them on several occasions. I particularly enjoyed spending time with her mother, who, I would learn, had the same kind of psychic intuition that my mom did.

I was home one night watching television when a vision—that's what I called them—hit me. I saw Gina in a car accident with a huge gash across her forehead. I immediately tried to reach her but got her mother instead. When we spoke, I learned she had seen the same vision I had. Unfortunately, our knowledge didn't help, and Gina was in the accident exactly as we had both seen it.

I left the hospital feeling despondent. I was tired of knowing things before they happened, and I was pissed off that I couldn't do anything to help.

On my way out of the hospital, I commanded:

> *Stop this. I do not want it anymore. I don't want to know what is going to happen before it happens. Put up the walls, block the flow, and stop the knowing—right now. I'm done. I command it, and so it is.*

I drove home.

I had asked the universe not to see any more. I was more than willing to give it all up.

9

Dating, the Peaceful Warrior and Writing and Becoming the List

After Gina recovered from her accident, I tried to make ours a romantic relationship, but she wasn't interested. Feeling ready now, I tried some dating. It wasn't easy. I tried to do some clubbing, but I was past the age when that was fun or rewarding. I did discover some great local rock bands during this time, and I got the chance to reconnect with my audio and singing talents.

I also met some interesting women—even if most of them were married, in a relationship, or thought I was too nice a guy to pursue a relationship with. When I finally did start to meet women who wanted more than to use my talents, they seemed to lose interest once it looked like the relationship could become serious.

I was experiencing a drought in my life for angels *and* women.

I continued to work long hours at Face Broadcast Productions. Occasionally I would help Jamie and Ron by picking up their son, Justin, from school. Over time, I became a mentor to him. The more we connected and spent time together, the more it seemed like he was shifting from the stereotypical negative teenager to a positive young man.

I asked him what had created such a dramatic shift in his energy. He told me that spending time with me had helped him, and I was happy to hear that. He also said that someone had given him a book that completely changed his life.

The next day he pulled me aside and said, "I finished the book. Somebody gifted this book to me, and now I realize that I am supposed to give it to you. Once you read it, please give it to somebody you care about."

He gave me *Way of the Peaceful Warrior,* by Dan Millman.

Like *Chicken Soup for the Soul,* the book changed how I was feeling and living my life. I started reading it every free moment I had.

The more I read, the more puzzled I became. There were so many similarities between this book and my time with John in Fresno; I wondered if somebody had been following me around taking notes!

Way of the Peaceful Warrior was a great read and initiated a profound shift in me. As instructed, I handed the book off to someone I cared about when I finished it—and promptly purchased my own copy.

I have come to understand that guiding forces are everywhere we go. They can be guardian angels, earthbound angels, or just a person you bump into at the coffee shop. These guides offer you keys that will help you open doors to new understanding—but you have to be receptive to make any use of them.

Rudy, the Law of Attraction, and the List

I had recently received guidance from Donna-Lisa and Justin, and my next guide would be a new co-worker at Face Broadcast Productions. He was a man named Rudy, whom I had interviewed and recommended hiring. We became good friends. One day, I was complaining to him about the women I was dating.

He laughed at me and said, "What do you expect?"

"I don't understand. Things start to go well—and then they dump me."

Then he asked me a question that changed everything: "What do you want?"

I didn't know how to answer.

He said, "There is this law of the universe, and it's called the Law of Attraction. It is as real as the law of gravity. What you say, what you think, or what you expect is what you will get, but only to the extent that you're clear about what you want. Because you have no idea what you want, you keep attracting women who don't know what *they* want. Does that make sense?"

It did. I asked him to tell me more.

He pointed out that, because of my guardian angel, my idea of the perfect woman was that one girl who had been pointed out to me. I never had the chance to make one up from scratch based on what I most wanted.

He said, "You have no idea what it's like to dream a woman up."

He was right.

Rudy explained further, "Keith, if you're going to order a pizza, you can put anything you want on that pizza. You can custom build it to be any way you want it, based on the toppings that you like. If you don't know what toppings you want, and you tell the pizza maker *I don't know—surprise me,* you're probably not going to get a pizza you like. You won't get the pizza that makes you happy. You have to get clear about what you really want, otherwise there's no way the perfect woman for you will find you."

Rudy suggested I go home that night, start with a blank sheet of paper, and ask myself these questions:

What do I want in my next relationship?

If the next person I meet is the person I'm going to be with for the rest of my life, what do I want her to be like?

What qualities will she have?

How will she act?

What will she like to do?

Where is she from?

What nationality is she?

What does she look like?

He told me to be very specific with the universe and honest with myself. He reminded me again that I could not attract what I wanted until I was clear what that was. He asked me to make the list, and bring it into work the next day. I agreed.

I went home that night, poured myself a drink, and pondered the questions. I sat there for hours creating an incredibly detailed list of what I wanted. It was an amazing and enlightening process. I realized that everything he had said was true. I had been completely out of touch with what I wanted for so long.

What did I want?

What a great question. It's something I should've considered before I even tried to start dating. I completed my list, and I couldn't wait to show Rudy the next day.

As soon as we got a chance, I showed him my list.

He read it over and said, "Great job. I think you should reword a few of these, but you're close. Go home, look at your list, and make sure you have included everything you want. You must make everything clear to the universe. Once you feel like you have it, I want you to pray to the God that you believe in, and believe that when you finish that prayer, the law of the universe will make it so. Then put the list away, and go back into life knowing that it's only a matter of time before this woman shows up. It's that easy."

I went home and continued to tweak my list. I made sure I was clear with the universe. My perfect mate would be willing to work at keeping the relationship fresh, was spiritual, giving, and would have all the qualities that were important to me, inside and out. My list was very detailed. I took my list, prayed on it, and put it away, knowing I would meet this woman when it was time.

That night, I put away what I now refer to as *The List,* and I prayed. I asked God to remove the walls I had put up, knowing I would never meet my perfect mate if I still had those walls up for my protection.

I asked God to reveal to me where I would meet this woman. After I asked the question, I went into *the silence*—a meditative state in which I had always received answers and visions in the past. I still use this process. I ask one question, sit and breathe in silence, and wait for the answer until it reveals itself to me.

As I sat breathing in and breathing out, I cleared my mind. All I could hear was my breath. My vision began with a remembrance of my first experience with the Agape International Spiritual Center. I had been attending services there for a few years now. I sat in quiet and relived many of the experiences I'd had at Agape, thinking about the beautiful music and some of the people I had met, including my musical mentor, Carl Anderson.

As I continued to breath, I pondered the question I had asked: *Where will I meet my perfect mate?*

I heard a voice whisper in my ear, "You will meet her at Agape."

It was so simply logical. I asked specifically for a like-minded beautiful woman whose light enters the room before she does.

Where else would I meet her?

There were two services offered at Agape each week. Once I knew I was going to meet the woman from my list at Agape, I decided to go to both services every week. This involved a very early wakeup call and a long day each Sunday, but I didn't want to sleep in one week, miss her, and then end up waiting longer to meet her. I had waited long enough.

Becoming the List

Before you read ahead, write your own list, thinking carefully about what you want and what you need in a partner. Search your heart. Be specific and be honest.

If you do this now, you will see something interesting when we get ahead a few pages.

Now, set the list aside, and read on.

Since discovering Agape in 1996, I had developed a regular meditation practice. Every day, I sat down in the silence to listen to what is referred to by many religions as *the still, small voice.*

After I wrote my list, I sat and pondered meeting this new woman of my dreams as I went into a meditative state.

My inner inquiry became this: *If the law of attraction mirrors what I am asking for, don't I need to be those things myself?*

Of course I do, I answered myself, and sighed.

Oh, this was going to require some work.

It is the flip side of the process; it is the other side of the coin.

It makes complete sense: How could I attract something that I am not, myself?

I heard a voice tell me: *Look at your list. Are you living the qualities you asked to attract?*

I opened my eyes, exhaled, and walked over to the drawer where I had placed my list.

Here is *The List*:

BEAUTIFUL, INSIDE AND OUT…

BEAUTIFUL, BROWN EYES

LONG, DARK HAIR

MEDIUM-TO-DARK SKIN

BIG NOSE

BIG BUTT

LOVES MUSIC

PLAYS GUITAR AND SINGS (NOT PROFESSIONALLY – JUST FOR FUN)

ARTIST/PAINTER

LOVES ME FOR WHO I AM

HONEST

HAS A GREAT SENSE OF HUMOR

GETS MY JOKES

LOVES MOVIES

OUTGOING

PASSIONATE

GIVING

CARES ABOUT OTHERS, AS WELL AS HERSELF

GIVES GREAT BACKRUBS

LOVES THE MOUNTAINS

ADVENTUROUS AND WILLING TO TRY NEW THINGS

HEALTHY, HAPPY DISPOSITION

GEOGRAPHICALLY DESIRABLE, OR WILLING TO RELOCATE

INNER STRENGTH

HAS A JOB

WILLING TO WORK AT KEEPING THE RELATIONSHIP FRESH

SPIRITUAL

LOVES BAREFOOT WALKS ON THE BEACH

PLAYFUL

SMOKE-FREE

DRINKS ALCOHOL OCCASIONALLY NOT PROFESSIONALLY

Note: Alcoholics were commonly referred to as professionals in show business and in my circles, so that explains the language I used in the last item on the list.

As I surveyed my list, I looked at the qualities I had listed.

After reading each item, I asked myself: *Am I that? Do I demonstrate that quality?*

A few items jumped out at me right away. If I was going to attract these qualities in a woman, there were three items to address right away.

The first was easy: SMOKE-FREE.

I had quit smoking cigarettes a long time ago, but perhaps it was time for me to give up the occasional pot smoking. I never really enjoyed how I felt when I smoked it, but my previous wife had loved it, so the habit had persisted through the years. Getting rid of something from my previous relationship seemed to be a smart way to open a place for my new one.

Next on the list was INNER STRENGTH.

I had overcome a lot in my life but in terms of relationships, I could see that I had let Rebecca run over me emotionally. It had been bad for me and for our relationship. I thought about the times I had let other people dictate situations in my life. I felt it was important for me to look at this quality and see what I could do to ramp up its manifestation.

The third and final item on my short list was HONEST.

This one was more of a challenge. I spent many days meditating on it.

I asked the universe: *Please reveal to me all the ways I was not, or am not, an honest man.*

A list was revealed to me:

- In your previous marriage
- About the break-up of your previous marriage
- In the way you lie for your bosses
- Why you lie in the first place

Never has such a short list said so much. I could see that there was important work to be done here. I decided, rather than trying to take on the whole list at once, I would take them one at time.

I Was Not Honest in My Previous Marriage

This one begged me to sit in meditation with it.

I sat, breathed the breath, and asked: *How was I not honest in my previous marriage?*

Nothing.

I took another series of breaths and asked again. Nothing. I continued to breathe in and out, and soon I drifted into a life review that played like a full feature movie on the screen of my mind.

The movie started way back in time, when I was just a child. It showed my guardian angel pointing out Rebecca to me and saying she would be my wife.

I saw a quick montage of all the times I had told my mother, "There's my future wife."

As I was watching, I had a sudden realization: My angel had told me she would be my wife, but he never said she would be my wife *forever*.

Rebecca was my wife, just as the angel had predicted, and we had loved each other and had tried to keep the marriage going.

I had determined that I was a failure because our relationship had ended. I was sure that I had let down both God and my guardian angel, but this was not the truth. I didn't fully understand what my angel had told me, but now it was clear.

I could see, now, that it was okay that our relationship hadn't lasted, and I could stop feeling like a failure. I had learned a lot about who I wanted to be, and, more important, who I did *not* want to be in my next relationship. In that moment, I realized that it had all happened perfectly, that I had not failed, and a heavy burden was lifted from my soul.

I Was Not Honest about the Break-up of My Previous Marriage

The next day, I sat down to meditate about the second thing on my list. This time, the words that came out in my vision were vague. I needed to ask this question in a way that would be productive and would provide answers. My inner guide told me I needed to break this one down into a few different questions.

I sat down and took many deep breaths to calm my mind. I took a few more to leave behind anything that had transpired before this meditation and to come fully into the present moment.

I asked a specific question: *Show me all the reasons I decided to end my relationship.*

Once again, I saw specific moments of my life in a movie format. I saw clips of Rebecca and me fighting. We were shouting at each other, saying hateful things that could never be taken back. There was a montage of doors slamming and images of us running away from each other. I saw the hell we put each other through.

I didn't know what seeing this movie was supposed to do for me. All I saw were good reasons for breaking up.

I received an answer: *Don't look at what happened. Think about why they happened.*

Still not understanding, I mused: *How was I supposed to know why she did what she did?*

The voice responded quickly: *Isn't it interesting—the words you use. You say, 'what she did,' as if you had no part in it whatsoever. Watch the movie again, and look for the why underneath the actions.*

The movie started again. I saw the clips of Rebecca and me fighting. This time, though, I also remembered all the arguments I had seen growing up—between my mother and my sister. Their fights looked exactly the same. There were different words, but the behavior was being repeated.

It was a revelation. I had taken this unhealthy behavior forward and was perpetuating it. I had dragged it with me, and I would continue to do that if I didn't make a change. I could choose alternatives. I could try other ways of communicating. I could read books and learn other strategies.

I realized that I could have tried these things when I was with Rebecca. I was responsible for my behavior in our relationship. It wasn't all her fault.

The movie continued and I was told: *Watch these moments, and discover what is underneath.*

Once again, I saw the montage of doors slamming and us running away from each other, repeatedly. This was painful to watch. As the scene ended, I thought of the words *running away*. Those two words just kept looping in my mind.

Yes, we ran away. Anyone could see that.

What was I supposed to do with this?

Look underneath the words. Why did you feel like you needed to run? Why didn't you stay and work it out?

I thought about these questions. I ran when I felt things were spinning out of control. When I watched those scenes from my life, I could still feel the intense fear that I had experienced in those moments. I realized something then. With Rebecca, I thought if I stayed longer, something awful or violent was going to happen.

Ah, yes. Be with that for a moment and watch this.

The life review movie started again. It was scenes of me punching holes in walls, throwing objects against the wall, hitting myself—all my violent outbreaks over the course of our relationship, strung together.

I started to get a little defensive. *Yeah, so what of it?*

Imagine yourself as a petite woman with a scared inner child. Imagine being with a strong and powerful man who has training in martial arts. Imagine watching him punch holes in walls like it's nothing. Imagine being Rebecca. What are you thinking?

I was silent.

You know what she would be thinking: He's a ticking time bomb. He could go off at any time. What if he decides to hit me next time instead of the wall?

How would that sit in your subconscious? What kind of reactions would it create inside of you? Now, imagine yourself as a child, seeing your father screaming at your mother, punching holes in walls, saying mean things, slamming the door, and leaving for hours at a time. You are just a child.

Don't you think that would scare you beyond belief? What might those memories create inside of you as a child?

I sat with those questions and insights for what must have been an hour, tears streaming down my cheeks. The scenes kept playing—over and over again.

I knew I wanted to be sure that I didn't take any of these issues into my next relationship. I also knew I needed to make amends to Rebecca and my son.

Welcome this awareness. Let it fill you.

The next movie scenes were about Rebecca's infidelities.

The first time was with someone I considered my best friend. I had encouraged him to hang out with Rebecca while I was at work. I had trusted him and felt betrayed by them. Every word out of my mouth in the big speech I spewed all over them was about what they did to me. After the movie stopped playing, I reviewed it in my mind and could see my part in what happened.

Basically, here is what I had said to my friend: *Here is my incredibly sexy, beautiful girlfriend. Hang out with her, drink with her, smoke with her—oh, but, whatever you do, even though you're a super horny teenager, don't touch her.*

Not my best move.

The second time was also with a friend. They were nudists. We all ended up partying naked, making out, and making love. There was only one bed in their apartment, and we went to sleep together. When Rebecca made a move on him while I was asleep, he told me immediately. Rebecca and I fought, and I played the victim. I could see now that I never gave her a chance to explain why she did what she did. It could have been unintentional. I would never know.

It was hard to watch.

Pointing fingers is much easier than taking personal responsibility, isn't it?

I could see that clearly now. I was ready for what was next.

Finally, I was shown scenes from the time when I was attending audio/video engineer school, and Rebecca accused me of not being there for her and our son.

In the movie scene, I was saying to Rebecca, "My getting a new career, one that will possibly pay really well and put me on my path, is exactly what support looks like. This is for you. I'm doing this for you."

The scene repeated. After seeing it several times, I noticed Rebecca pleading for attention, pleading for support with our son, pleading for me to make time to be with them. The audio/video program was six months long. This was a long time for a wife to have her husband absent. It was a long time for a little boy to have his father absent.

When the movie continued, I watched how, after graduation, my job in TV production took me away up to sixty hours a week, plus commuting time. By the time Rebecca cheated the third time, I had been focused on nothing but work for about a year and a half. I had been spending no time with them at all.

In these scenes, everything was about *me,* and for *me,* no matter how I tried to spin it. Rebecca had begged and pleaded for me to give her any kind of notice. In the end, she chose to do something that would definitely get my attention. The part I had played in this story was easy to see.

I sat in the silence, in the darkness, hearing nothing but the sound of my breath. The movie was over; I had learned what I needed to learn.

I Was Not Honest in the Way I Lied for My Bosses

I already understood what this one was about, but I watched the life review movie anyway. It showed me how many times I had been asked to lie for my bosses. There were little lies, like saying they weren't available when they actually didn't want to talk to someone, or misrepresenting why some job was overlooked on a project or deadline.

It didn't take me long to know what my next steps needed to be. I continued to breathe into the ways I would present my case and choose how I would respond to multiple scenarios of what their reaction might be.

That day I went to work and told Jamie and Ron and the two other assistants that I needed to talk with them.

When everyone was present, I said, "I will not lie for you anymore. If you don't want to talk to a salesperson because you're editing, I will tell them you can't be interrupted when you are editing. I will not tell them you will call them later, if I know this isn't true. There are a lot of ways I can handle the calls and still tell the truth. This is the only thing I have an interest in doing. I will not lie if a mistake is made, and I will not lie if I make a mistake. People make mistakes. We're dealing with a lot here, and we are human. There is no reason to lie. Imagine how it would look if we were caught in a lie? What would that say about our company? If you have an issue with this, fire me now. I would also appreciate it if you gave these assistants permission to tell the truth as well."

Jamie and Ron not only accepted what I shared, but they gave all employees the go ahead to be honest. They thanked me for considering our reputation as a company in my speech. It couldn't have gone better.

I Was Not Honest About Why I Lie in the First Place

The next day, I went into meditation wondering how long I had been lying. I asked to go back in time to see examples so I could put them into perspective.

This movie started in my childhood. Because of my mother's illnesses and our poverty, I often lied about our situation to avoid being made fun of. By junior high, lying was a regular practice. I had nothing going on in my life that could compare with the rich kids, so I lied whenever I thought there was a need. Lying was a way to get around what I felt was the embarrassing truth of my home life.

The more I saw, the more I realized that I lied when I was in a situation in which I felt inferior or embarrassed. When I came out of this meditation, I made a list of situations in which I was currently lying and began immediately to correct these situations.

After this, I tracked down people—some of whom I hadn't spoken to in some time—to make amends for my dishonesty. It was like carrying out my own *Liars Anonymous* program. It was a lot of work, but worth every minute of it. Each time I spoke with someone, I felt a little freer.

I noticed that I was starting to more directly experience some of the other listed qualities such as INNER STRENGTH and BEAUTIFUL, INSIDE AND OUT.

I was *becoming* The List.

Gaining Understanding and Making Amends

At that time, John Gray's *Men Are from Mars, Women Are from Venus: The Classic Guide to Understanding the Opposite Sex* was sitting on top of the bestseller lists. I assumed it was another man-bashing book until I was encouraged to read it by a male friend. I'm glad I did. I couldn't believe how much I loved this book. It defined how men act in relationships—ways I had not noticed. What I thought were just my quirky issues, unique to me, I learned were common issues for other men. It was a relief—and an eye opener.

The book also defined women, how they think, what they want, and the best way to speak with them. This part of the book was enlightening and life changing. I started to see some of the mistakes I had made with women in the past. I learned the importance of listening, rather than doing, when a woman talked.

I wished I had accessed this information fifteen years earlier!

I came to understand that men and women are completely different, and that was okay. If I stood a chance of ever pulling off another relationship, it was of utmost importance that I learn to understand how women see the world, how to listen to them, and how to be supportive and loving.

Not long after finishing this book, I was able to meet up with Rebecca. She had been taking Timar to visit with her periodically, and after one visit, she brought him home and stayed in the area for a few days to visit her family and some friends. I met them at the airport.

I had an opportunity to make amends, to be honest, and to make more strides towards becoming my list, but I knew it wouldn't be easy.

I looked Rebecca in the eyes and said, "I have something I need to tell you. Please let me talk until I am finished."

"Okay, go right ahead."

I told her about all I had read and learned over the past months, and finally, I owned my part in what had happened between us. I asked for her forgiveness. She was crying when I finished, and she thanked me for what I had said. We were finally able to be friends again. We were able to forge a loving connection, even if we couldn't be together the way we had envisioned.

This was the last major piece of becoming The List.

Sighing with relief, and feeling profoundly unburdened, I stepped into living my life in faith, knowing that when the time was right, I would meet the woman of my dreams, my perfect mate, the one I had dreamed up and ordered from the universe. It was going to happen.

There was nothing to do now but sit back, enjoy my life, and wait for her to arrive.

10

Beauty Enters the Room

Around this time, Timar, who was missing his mother, asked if he could go live with her for the next school year. Rebecca and I agreed to let him try it out. Meanwhile, I continued to attend both services each week at Agape. On August 8, 1999, approximately six months after I made my list, I completed Agape's new member course.

This day was particularly special for me because the recent graduates would be honored and formally introduced to the community. We stepped up, one at a time, and said our names over the microphone, while people kept up a constant flow of clapping. It was a wonderful ritual. After this, we headed to our assigned seats for the day.

After services were complete, I stood up to greet Benjamin, a congregant I had connected with during the course. As I hugged Benjamin, my attention was captured by a light across the room. Inside this bright light was the most beautiful woman.

She was walking our way. She had long dark straight hair, big brown eyes. I thought she looked Italian—or else she had a great tan. She had a big nose. She had what appeared to be a big booty. To me, it was like there was a neon sign hanging over her head with arrows pointing down to her, and a sign flashing: *It's HER*!

When she got to us, Benjamin said, "Maura," and engulfed her in a big hug.

I knew that Benjamin was gay, so she wasn't with him.

Benjamin introduced us, and I managed to say, "Hi."

I couldn't keep my eyes off her.

Benjamin continued by saying, "I met Maura at the community living center I've been staying at. Maura is a singer, and I keep telling her she should sing here at Agape. Maura, Keith is singing here next week. Maybe he could help you audition."

She said she couldn't make it the next week because she was working, but I got her number. We made a promise to each other that we'd find a way to connect and work together at a later date.

Let the Love Begin

I saw her a few days later at Benjamin's house. I was giving him a guitar lesson when she dropped by. I can still see her. She was wearing a purple sundress, and her hair was down to below her perfect butt. She wore no shoes and no bra. She looked so hot.

I tried to play it cool. I managed to contain myself enough that Maura didn't notice, but Benjamin did. I couldn't get her out of my head. She was the woman I had ordered from the universe. I was going to spend the rest of my life with her, I knew it, but I wasn't going to blow it by coming on too strong. I was also committed to The List, and I needed to learn some more about her.

On August 15, which was my birthday, I sang at Agape for the first time. I tried to call Maura during the following week but kept getting her answering machine. Toward the end of the week, she called and let me know that she had been away all week, assisting at a seminar.

She invited me for the closing ceremony of the seminar. I wrote down the information and made plans to be there.

At the ceremony, when they opened the door to let guests in, I saw her. She was glowing. Seeing her again took my breath away. She was at the door handing out candles to people.

She saw me and said, "Keith, what are you doing here?"

I reminded her that she had invited me. Apparently, she had invited me in her message because she felt bad about not being available for my calls, but she didn't actually expect me to come.

After everyone entered the room, the lights went out. The seminar facilitator started to share a story, but I was surveying the room looking for Maura, so I wasn't paying much attention to the process. Soon, the facilitator took his lit candle and lit someone else's, then everyone starting passing it on by lighting each other's candles. I had spotted Maura and headed her way. She got her candle lit just before I arrived.

As I was standing in front of her, she looked deep into my eyes with a big smile on her face, and then lit my candle. Soon, every candle in the room was lit. The facilitator completed the process, everyone celebrated the grads, and I headed out. Maura had to stay behind to clean up, but she said she would catch up with me.

All I could think of was how she had looked so deep into my eyes with that beautiful smile and I thought to myself: *Oh yeah, she's into me*!

I didn't find out until later that this wasn't exactly what was happening in that moment.

Do you remember when, during the introduction to the closing ceremony, I wasn't paying attention to the facilitator because I was looking for Maura?

You may get a good laugh from this funny fact: I didn't hear the facilitator telling everyone that when you lit someone's candle, you were to look into their eyes, and see the beauty of who they are. Everyone was doing it.

I didn't find this out until much later when I shared the story with Maura of how I thought she was in love with me from the start.

The next day, Benjamin called to tell me he'd mentioned my interest to Maura but she was not looking for a boyfriend, or to be in relationship. She wasn't looking for anything other than friendship.

He asked, "Are you okay with that?"

I smiled, "Any minute I get to spend with Maura will be a minute well spent. I'm not insisting on starting a dating relationship. If we spend time together as friends, I will consider each moment a blessing. I'm fine with it."

I knew the truth. I had done the work I needed to do, and if she was indeed the person I thought she was, nothing could stop this relationship. Maura and I connected on the phone a few days later and spoke for just over two hours. We kept finding subjects to talk about and agreed on so many things.

Finally, I sensed it was time for me to test the waters.

I asked her if she'd like to go out with me on a date.

My heart pounded as I waited for her answer.

She said, "Sure."

Our First Three Dates

First, we set a date for Friday. After talking for a while, Maura discovered she was also free on Monday. By this point, neither of us wanted to give up the Friday date, so we decided we would schedule both days. It turned out that the Wednesday in between the dates, Maura needed help moving, so we ended up having what we now call the *three first dates.*

Date #1

The whole weekend, I was nervous and excited about Monday. I was feeling like a teenager. I told my bosses at Face that I needed to make sure I got off on time that day, in plenty of time to pick up Maura. I got off work, jumped in my car, drove just a few miles, and—

My car broke down.

No!

Can you imagine my panic?

I tried to calm myself down. I paced back and forth next to the car. How long I had been looking forward to this first date, this *beginning*. I'd been waiting for Maura for so long.

Thinking about waiting for Maura made me remember The List. I stopped pacing.

INNER STRENGTH.

Yes.

I quieted myself down and looked inward: *Angels, tell me what to do.*

I heard: *Go to Rudy.*

Since he was the reason I had written The List in the first place, I thought this was a good sign. He lived nearby, so I ran to his place as fast as I could. I told him what had happened and asked if he would drive me to the closest rental car place so I could keep my date.

He said, "Here, take my car," and tossed me his keys.

I called Maura, telling her I was running late and why. She told me not to worry about it and asked me to drive safely. I drove for what felt like hours, while taking all the short cuts I knew. Somehow, not only was I there in time, but I was a tad early. I decided I would stop off at the flower shop and see what they had. I bought her one long stem yellow rose.

I arrived at Maura's house and parked, but, before I got out of the car, I gave myself some good advice: *Okay, relax, you've got this. Take your time. You know she's the one, but she doesn't yet know you are the one. Be cool.*

I stepped up to the door with rose in hand and knocked.

Maura opened the door and invited me in. She was living in a house that looked like it was inhabited by many roommates.

Maura looked at me and said, "Would you like something to drink?" and then she whispered softly, "Say no."

I was puzzled, but I followed along. I politely—and loudly—declined her offer.

She showed me around the place and then whispered, "Get me out of here, please."

We exited the building and she told me about her living situation. It was a group home, and it was owned by a man who had a booth down at the Venice Beach boardwalk. He was kind of a political radical who had money. He had purchased a few houses, gutted them out, and set them up so that he could give reasonable housing to large groups of people. He offered them a roof over their head and perhaps, for some of them, a stepping stone toward getting a place of their own.

Maura had been told that it was a spiritual community—like an ashram—but once she moved in, she had discovered that it was much more like a drug den filled with transient and mentally unstable individuals.

I took Maura down to the boardwalk of Venice Beach, and we found a nice restaurant. At first, we sat outside so we could enjoy the sunset as we ordered our food. The sun set quickly, and before our food arrived, we moved inside. Most of our conversation was about our past relationships, growing up, our families, and, for me, my work situation. One nice surprise was that Maura was actually eating. I was so used to California girls who didn't ever seem to eat.

Not only did Maura enjoy her meal, but also, at one point, she started looking with interest at *my* plate.

At one point, after asking, "Are you going to eat that?" she promptly grabbed a piece of my dinner and stuck it in her mouth.

I was so turned on.

Other than some confusion around paying for the bill—I'd left my wallet in the car, forgot to get cash, and had to use a pay phone to activate a new credit card—it was a perfect meal. As I pondered what to do next, I spotted Pacific Park on the Santa Monica Pier. We decided that would be our next destination.

While in line for the roller coaster, I stood behind Maura. I remember aching to kiss her, but I held back. The ride was great, and I liked that Maura seemed to have no fear. We went to the giant Ferris wheel next. When we got to the high point of the revolution, and the car was teetering, I was listening to Maura talk, watching the wind blow through her long hair, and I, again, wanted to kiss her so badly it hurt.

Patience, I told myself.

As we walked past a restaurant, I asked Maura if she wanted to go in and see what was happening in the bar. We popped our heads in, and there was a solo musician singing the Eagles song, *Take it Easy*.

I asked Maura, "Shall we?"

She nodded, and we found ourselves a seat, which wasn't too difficult since there was only one other couple in the whole place. We sat and listened to the musician as he worked his way through his top-forty rock repertoire. After a few songs, I moved my chair around to sit right next to Maura. I took my seat, and I put my arm around her. My heart was pounding quickly, and I could feel my pulse in my neck.

Maura told me later that when I put my arm around her, there were fireworks going off in her head, like the beginning of the seventies television show, *Love American Style*. It was at this point she realized she was attracted to me. Before this, she thought I was a nice guy, and figured we'd be friends, but had not been aware of any chemistry between us.

A few heart-pounding songs later, the musician took a break. I excused myself to go to the restroom. I saw the soloist there.

I pulled out a ten-dollar bill and asked him, "During your next set, will you allow me to step up and play a song for the girl I'm with? We are on our first date. She's never heard me play or sing."

He smiled, took the money, and said, "You got it."

When I returned to Maura, the other couple had left the bar, so it was just a bartender, the musician, and us. We continued to talk easily until the musician returned to play his next set.

After a few songs, he looked at me and said, "You want to come on up and sing a song for your date?"

I smiled at Maura, headed over to the musician, strapped on his guitar, and stepped up to the mic.

"This is a song I wrote some time ago. It's called *Forever.*"

I had written this song for my ex-wife. I know what you're thinking—it doesn't seem fitting to sing a song that I wrote for another woman, but I was acting on instinct at this point—or perhaps, on an angel's unspoken advice. In any case, I had no doubt about the song choice. Not only did the song seem appropriate for the moment; it truly felt relevant.

Some of the lyrics of the song are:

> *As I look into your eyes, I see the future. And when I look closer, girl, I see forever in your eyes . . . and way back when, I had a vision . . . that you and I, you and I, we'd last forever.*

It was a gutsy call, but I went for it. Maura responded in kind by stepping up, strapping on the guitar, and singing a song to me. She was so adorable. She managed to make her way through the song, and I clapped out loud for her.

She had just demonstrated one more of the things on The List: PLAYS GUITAR AND SINGS (NOT PROFESSIONALLY—JUST FOR FUN). As we connected and swapped likes, dislikes, and stories, I had been checking in with The List inside of my head. I was mentally checking things off:

LOVES MUSIC

ARTIST/PAINTER

HAS A GREAT SENSE OF HUMOR

GETS MY JOKES

OUTGOING

ADVENTUROUS AND WILLING TO TRY NEW THINGS

SPIRITUAL

PLAYFUL

SMOKE-FREE

DRINKS ALCOHOL OCCASIONALLY NOT PROFESSIONALLY

PLAYS GUITAR AND SINGS (NOT PROFESSIONALLY—JUST FOR FUN)

We were off to a great start!

A few songs later, I realized it was getting late. As much as I wanted to stay out all night with this goddess, I knew I had to return the car to Rudy, and it was a long drive after I dropped her off at her place. We drove to her place, and I walked her up to the door. She turned around to face me.

Again with the inner dialogue: *Okay, here we go. What to do? Tongue or no tongue? Don't blow this.*

I heard my guardian angel say: *Just trust yourself. You will make the right choice.*

I said to Maura, "I had a really great time tonight."

"Me too."

"So, we're still on for Friday night?"

"Yes."

"You want to go see a movie?"

"Sounds great."

"Want me to choose it?"

"Sure, that works for me."

"Okay. So, I guess I should go. I have to get up pretty early."

"I understand."

I looked into Maura's beautiful eyes, leaned forward, and gave her three quick kisses on the lips.

I said, "Good night," then slowly turned and headed toward the car.

Inside, I was jumping up and down, pumping my fist!

However, on the outside, I continued to act cool until I had entered the car, strapped myself in, and driven out of sight. All the way home to Rudy's house, I sang, played drums on the steering wheel, and offered a prayer of gratitude for such a wonderful first date. This was the greatest first date ever.

Date #2

Maura and I now refer to this day as our second date, but it wasn't planned as a date. Maura was moving, and she needed help. She didn't have much to move, and she had no car. I offered to help, borrowed Rudy's car again, and drove over to the house. Benjamin was there when I arrived, and together, the three of us loaded up the car with Maura's belongings. Rudy's car was a two-seater sports car with some room behind the seats, and it had a hatchback. Once we filled up the back with Maura's things, there was only room for two in the car.

Benjamin, grinning wickedly at us, agreed to stay behind.

As we left, he called out, "I know what you two are going to do."

When we arrived at Maura's new place, we met her new roommate. He walked us around the inside of the house. It was filled with the belongings of a handful of other roommates.

He walked us to a garage that had been turned into a bedroom and said, "This is you."

We made a few trips back and forth from car to room. On the third trip, when I went out to the car to retrieve another box, Maura was leaning up against the car, waiting for me, with a beautiful smile on her face.

She said, "You know, if we're going to be accused of making out, we might as well do it."

I had to agree, and we starting kissing like two kids discovering love for the first time. A rush surged through my body. From then on, as we continued to move boxes, we took frequent kissing breaks. On the last trip, we took a bit of a longer kiss break. Soon, we decided we'd better get back to our waiting friend.

When we returned to Benjamin, he smiled at us, saying, "Hmmm, didn't expect to see you two again for a long time."

We loaded up the car again, said goodbye to Benjamin, and headed back for more—moving!

Date #3

For the rest of the week, all I could think about was our next date. I still had transportation problems. Rudy needed his car on Friday, and mine was still at the shop. With the help of my employers at Face, I went out on my lunch break and rented a car.

Renting a car, just for a date?

It wasn't a hard decision to make; there wasn't anything more important to me at this time than being with Maura. My efforts weren't wasted—I could tell Maura was impressed that I had thought to rent a car just for our date.

After I had picked her up, when we were on our way to the movie, she said, "Is this car an automatic?"

"Yes."

I wondered: *Why did she want to know?*

I asked her, and she replied, "If it's an automatic, you can keep your hand on my leg the whole time."

Grinning as I placed my hand on her leg, I thought: *This is going to be one great date.*

I did not remove my hand from her leg until we arrived at the movie theatre parking lot. I was so loving this woman!

We went to see *The Muse,* but I don't remember much of the movie because Maura and I were making out for most of it. After the credits had finished rolling—waiting until movie credits were over before leaving was one more thing we had in common—we walked out hand in hand, stopping now and then to kiss some more. In the parking lot, I realized I couldn't remember where we parked. Maura couldn't remember either.

The rental tag on the keys told us we were looking for a silver car, but all the kissing we kept doing distracted us from finding the vehicle.

Finally, Maura sat down, and with a cute smile on her face, she said, "Okay, so all this kissing is obviously taking our brains away. We will never find the car this way. We have to stop kissing until the car has been located."

It was hard, but we managed stop kissing long enough for our brains to begin working. I looked at the key tag again and discovered that it had the make, model, and license plate number right there on the tag. We continued our search with this newly discovered information and finally, we found the car.

Turns out, they had put the wrong car color on the tag. With all our attention focused on touching each other, neither of us had noticed that the car we'd been driving was not actually silver—it was metallic blue!

Once in the car, Maura asked if she could see my place. I told her my nephew was there spending time with his girlfriend, since he was leaving for college in a few days. If she didn't mind company, it was fine with me.

We arrived at my apartment, and after I made introductions, Maura looked at me and asked, "Where is your room?"

"At the end of the hallway," I replied, and I waved to my nephew and his girl as Maura took my hand and led me toward my room.

I love this woman, I thought again to myself.

I excused myself to the bathroom, and when I came back, Maura was laying on the bed. She looked at me and patted the bed with her hand. I joyfully and gratefully obliged.

We made love for the first time that night, and we fell asleep snuggling, with Maura on my arm. When I woke, I was surprised. I had never been able to get to sleep if someone was on my arm like that. It was truly a first.

I woke up first, and I just laid there as still as I could, looking down at her beautiful face as she continued to sleep. When I tried to pull my arm back, Maura woke up.

"Good morning, beautiful," I said.

"Good morning. Did I sleep the whole night on your arm?"

"Yes. And that's a first. I've never been able to sleep in that position."

"I hope you don't think any less of me for inviting you to bed like that and staying the night."

"Of course not," I said.

"Great, because I really like you. I care about what you think about me."

It was a wonderful night and a wonderful morning. The warmth and joy of being with Maura filled my heart.

Yes, that just happened. Boom! I wanted to yell to the world.

Inseparable

Over the next two weeks, I stayed at Maura's new place, sleeping with her on the floor. She typically slept in a hammock, but the two of us couldn't sleep in it. She chose to join me on the floor, covered with a sleeping bag and a blanket. I wasn't sleeping very well, but I didn't care.

Every morning, I would wake up, take a shower with Maura, get dressed, and drive her to work. Next, I would jump on the freeway and spend the next forty-five minutes driving the eight miles to my job.

Forty-five minutes for only eight miles? Is that a typo, you ask?

Nope, that's a California freeway commute.

After work, I'd go through the process in reverse. We would go somewhere to get dinner and then head to her place. We would watch TV occasionally, but spent most of our time trying to catch up on a lifetime missed. We would retire to the floor, make love, and go to sleep. The next day we would get up and do it all again.

About a week into my staying with her at her place, she asked, "Do you want to do secrets?"

I wasn't sure I liked the sound of that. Certain truths had permanently damaged some of my past relationships.

I hedged, "What do you mean, do I want to 'do secrets'?"

"It feels as though things are getting serious here, so would you like to play a game called *Secrets,* in which we tell each other everything, all the deepest darkest secrets that we've never told anyone else?"

"Are you sure you really want to play that game with me? I've already told you some of my past. My life is filled with a lot of drama and a lot of dark things. I mean, truly, do you really want to go there?"

"Yes, it's important to me."

"Okay—you go first."

Maura shared all her secrets with me. It didn't take her very long, and her secrets were really nothing too shocking to me.

When she was finished, she looked at me and said, "Your turn."

I took a deep breath and thought: *Here we go.*

I was sure that this particular game of hers would be the end of us. There were bound to be some deal breakers that would come out, and then she would be gone.

Inner strength, I thought, sadly. *Inner strength and honesty.*

I knew if I wanted to keep pursuing this relationship, it would have to be this way.

I must have looked worried, because Maura took my hand and assured me everything would be okay. I went all in, and told her everything. The intensity of my secrets had us both in tears. We held each other, and it was clear that this process had done nothing but bring us closer together.

We spent every spare moment together for weeks, and it was the best time of my life.

When my nephew left for college one morning, I arranged a full day off, my first in over fifteen years. I felt like I was due to have a Keith day.

I should spend some time by myself, shouldn't I?

Everyone needs that alone time, right?

Well, I tried. By afternoon, I was on the phone telling Maura how much I missed her. I asked her if she would come over.

She asked, "Are you sure?"

I said, "Yes baby, I miss you so bad."

By bus, it took her a couple of hours to get to me, but she came.

She ended up staying for good.

We had been living together for about a week when Maura said, "You know, there are three words we have not said to each other."

"I know. Every time I have said those words first, it didn't work out well for me."

"Yeah, the same goes for me. How about if we come up with a code word instead?"

"What do you mean?"

"When either of us is ready—and really, only when one of us is truly ready—we can say something like, *french fries*."

We agreed that that is what we would do. A few days passed.

"Keith?"

"Yes, Maura."

"French fries."

I smiled from ear to ear and replied, "French fries."

And to this day, if you go and find my calendar from the year 1999, you will see written on this date: *MAURA AND I ARE IN FRIES*.

We went with those words for a while. It may seem strange to you, but it worked for us. I can't remember which one of us finally broke down and said the words *I love you*, but by the time it happened, neither one of us was afraid of it.

The Proposal

Maura had moved to California from New England in part because she had heard about Agape and was interested in checking it out. She had lived in California for a few years when she was young and had always felt pulled to return. On a whim, she packed up a few things and moved to California. Upon her arrival, she found a place to live in the so-called ashram, and became part of Agape community. She met many new people, who would invariably ask her what prompted her move.

She said that it always seemed right to say in response, "I came for the sunshine."

On our third date, when she told me this story, I stood there in silence, with my eyes welling up.

Maura looked at me and said, "What's the matter?"

"My mother has always called me her Son-shine. You came here for the Son-shine all right. You came here for me."

When I took Maura to meet my mother, for the first time in my life, my mother approved of my mate. Mom had always been super possessive of me, and had not approved of any woman I had ever brought home; she never thought any of them were worthy of her Son-shine, until Maura.

When I told Maura about my list, I learned she went through almost the same process. Instead of making a list, she had *a relationship plan*. She gave it to me to read.

I couldn't stop smiling as I read it. It was as if she had followed me around for months taking notes. Just as Maura had everything on my list, everything in her relationship plan applied directly to me.

A few days later, Maura and I were at the mall, and we passed a jewelry store. We were looking at rings, and she told me she didn't like diamonds. She said if she ever received an engagement ring, she would prefer a pearl like her mother had. I was thinking what a blessing this was, as pearls are far less expensive than diamonds. Plus, the thought of buying a diamond engagement ring pushed buttons for me—and brought back bad memories. Everything about this woman was perfect, down to her ring choice. As we continued looking at rings, she found a ring with a pearl that had a little ruby next to it.

She pointed to it and said, "If I were going to get an engagement ring, I would want one like that one."

In my mind, she had just given me the go-ahead, and I couldn't have been happier. She had even matter-of-factly told me which ring I should give her. To this day, she denies that she was hinting I should give her that ring or propose to her. Because, in her mind, she was far from ready.

I was *more* than ready, however.

Within the week, I went to the mall and purchased the ring. I took a guess at her finger size, hoping that I was right. The owner of the store assured me that we could bring it to them and have it sized either way upon our return.

Soon after I purchased the ring, we were invited to spend Christmas in Vermont with her family. Finally, I was going to meet her mom and dad.

As soon as I heard about the invitation, I thought to myself: *What a great opportunity to propose to her*!

I thought there would be no better place to propose than in the same bed she slept in when she dreamed of marriage as a teenager; where she imagined her Prince Charming as a child. I would propose to her at her house, in that room, while she was in that bed. I couldn't wait.

We took a nonstop red-eye flight from LAX to Boston, which gave us both a serious case of jetlag. We would need to take a bus from Boston to a town in Vermont about an hour away from her parents' house, where her mother would pick us up. We had some time to kill before our bus would arrive, so Maura took me for a ride on the T—the mass transit subway in Boston. This was new for me, as I had never been on anything that even resembled a subway or a tramway.

We walked along the Charles River. There was snow, and it was magical, although it was freezing cold. Being from California, I was enjoying the novelty immensely. Maura didn't feel the same way about the cold and snow, but we wandered about happily, hand in hand. She was just so beautiful, red-cheeked in the cold, eyes full of love. It took everything inside of me to not change plans and ask her to marry me then and there.

I asked myself: *Should I propose now?*

Checking with my angels within, I was told to stick to the plan.

We took the bus to White River Junction, where her mother met us and drove us to their house deep in the Northeast Kingdom of Vermont. When we arrived at the house, Maura's father greeted us at the door. Maura and I were both beyond sleepy; we were ready for a nap. Her mom noticed and suggested we head upstairs to catch up on some sleep before dinner, assuring us that they would still be there when we woke up. We gratefully went upstairs and face-planted on Maura's bed.

We slept for about three hours. I woke up first and grabbed the ring I had purchased for this exact moment. I had the ring in my hand as I knelt next to Maura and waited for her to wake up.

I commanded myself to be patient. She looked so peaceful sleeping there. I basked in her beauty and, as she slept and dreamed, I imagined what she had looked like when she was a girl. I was beyond grateful that I had listened to Rudy, put the law of attraction to work, and attracted this perfect mate to me.

I couldn't believe how fast I had come to the decision to ask her to marry me. Truth be told, after my divorce, I was quite sure I would never marry again. Meeting and dating Maura had completely changed my mind. I listened to her breathing while she slept, and it reminded me of every breath I had taken in meditation, every step I had taken to become the man she deserved. I knew I was her match too. I had seen her list.

It was a match made in heaven, *and if she would ever wake up, I would finally have my chance to bring this proposal home.*

Finally, she rolled over and began to wake. I was on my knees, ready to go.

When she opened her eyes, there I was with the ring box open.

I said, "Maura, will you marry me?"

Sleepily, she mumbled, "What are you doing?"

"Um, I'm proposing to you. Let me try this again."

I slipped the ring on her finger and spoke the words I had so carefully planned out.

"I wanted you to be in the bed where you dreamed up your Prince Charming when I proposed to you. Maura, my love, will you honor me by becoming my wife?"

Her eyes widened and she said, "What are you thinking? We just got here. My dad is going to kill you!"

The expression on her face was hard to read. There was love there, but also a great deal of something that looked like *alarm*.

I tried to smile, "Okay, this is getting weird now. Will you marry me or not?"

"I have to talk to my sister."

What?

So much for my perfect plan.

She got up and dressed, stuck her hand in her pocket, and took off downstairs. I followed her. She grabbed her mother and headed into the bathroom. Her father was looking at me sideways, quizzically.

The next few hours were a bit uncomfortable.

Are you worried, reader?

Let me reassure you—it all turned out well!

Maura received the green light from her mother, and after speaking with her sister on the phone, got the second green light. She brought me back to the bedroom and—joy!—gave me an official *yes* to my proposal.

Her father, in his old-school Italian way, was trying to process what on earth had just happened in his home. He didn't even know my full name yet, and I had already put a ring on his daughter's finger. In retrospect, perhaps I should have gotten to know him for a day or two.

Perhaps I should have asked for his blessing first?

I could only hope that he would understand that I was too much in love with his daughter to wait. We were ready, now, to set sail into the future together.

11

A Stress-Free, Fairy-Tale Wedding

Maura's mother immediately went into wedding-plan mode. The rest of our visit to Vermont was filled with the family getting to know me, me getting to know them, wedding ceremony discussions—and lots and lots of cheese.

Cheese?

Yes, you read it right—cheese.

Maura's family is Italian, and during the holidays, every meal, every dessert, even breakfast, involved some type of cheese. This food was so good I was gaining weight just looking at it. It was a fantastic Christmas for me in every way.

Maura was enjoying being engaged. She had waited a long time to meet a man who was worthy of her love. She had worked hard to become the person she needed to be, to attract me into her life. She was grateful, and it was obvious by the way she looked at me, the way she treated me, and the love that she showed me daily.

Every person we spent time with was inspired by our connection. It was so obvious how in love we were, and how respectful we were with each other. Remarkably, we were communicating well too. Neither one of us was quite sure how or why, but we loved it. Every time something came up that would have been a huge fight in past relationships, we were able to talk it out, and fix any problem that arose.

Everyone was having fun getting involved in the planning of our wedding. One of the TV producers I had become great friends with offered up her beautiful home for our wedding shower.

She said, "Don't you worry about cost, food, or the place; I've got all that covered."

And she did. Our shower was beautiful and well attended by friends.

It didn't take me long to realize that Maura was planning a fairy-tale wedding. Everything about our relationship resembled a fairy tale: the way we met, my proposal, and the way we were with each other. Maura figured it made sense to continue with that theme.

It wasn't long before she asked me if I would dress up like a prince.

For some reason—you can see it *must* have been true love!—I agreed.

Back in California, we went to a costume shop in Hollywood. A woman named Genevieve assisted us at the shop. She not only helped us pick out our wedding outfits, and assisted us with the fittings, but she became a good friend as well.

We even had fairy-tale wedding invitations, which included, of course, a fairy-tale story:

> *Prince Keith and Princess Maura*
>
> *Once upon a time, there lived a beautiful princess named Maura. Princess Maura had a wonderful, joyful life, but she longed for a handsome prince to share her life with. She searched far and wide, and met many fine gentlemen, but none that she could call her prince. Then one day, the angels had a meeting and decided it was time for Princess Maura to meet her prince.*

The only trouble was they forgot to tell the princess.

And so, when Prince Keith arrived, all ready to sweep Princess Maura off her feet and take her away to the married people's kingdom, Princess Maura said, "Thank you anyway. You seem like a fine young man, but I've grown tired of searching for my prince, and have decided to enjoy my life alone."

Prince Keith was undaunted. He had been told by the angels that Princess Maura was to be his wife, and when he saw how beautiful she was, he was overcome with joy, and he knew that nothing would stand in the way of their union. Well, it didn't take Princess Maura very long to realize that Prince Keith was in fact the very one she had searched for, prayed for, and dreamed of for so long. He was here at last, and he was even more wonderful than she had imagined.

And so, a royal wedding was announced, complete with family, friends, and festivities...

Maura set an intention around the planning of our wedding.

She said, "Our wedding day is going to be special and it's going to be stress-free. The way we get married will set the tone for the rest of our relationship, and no one is going to mess with that."

And, make no mistake—she was serious about this.

If anyone tried to bring stress into our vision, they were fired. Maura hired and fired the baker, then the florist, and we almost eloped when her mother started to bring stress into the process.

A woman I worked with at Face Broadcast recommended an Italian restaurant she had frequently visited. She had seen a wedding held there and thought it would be a great location for our wedding, so she gave me the name of one of the owners, and told me to mention her name when we visited. Maura and I went and checked it out, and it was exactly as she said—only better.

There was a nice space in between the restaurant and the building next door that seemed like the ideal spot for an outdoor wedding. The parking structure behind the two buildings had a flight of stairs that led to the entrance. There was an elevator to the left and to the right of the downstairs entrance. These elevators led to the upper floors of the structure.

Using a little bit of imagination, this parking structure could easily double as a castle, where a prince and princess might live. We decided this was the perfect location.

We met with the owners and tried the food. It was wonderful. When it came to the cost, we received their family deal because of the referral. We still cannot believe how little they charged us and how well they treated us.

We did nearly everything ourselves. Because I was an audio/video engineer, I chose the music, created CDs, and planned the lineup of music for our wedding and reception. The bass player of my band acted as disc jockey.

We sent out the invitations with the fairy-tale theme, but did not tell anyone how we would be dressed at the wedding. The seats were set between the two buildings, facing the parking garage. As we got ready to begin, all our guests were in their seats, visiting and having fun, none the wiser as to what we were about to do.

The wedding started with medieval sounding bugles, and at the top of his register, a friend proclaimed, while pointing up to the top of the parking garage, "Look, up there!"

Everyone stopped and looked up to see Prince Keith and Princess Maura, up on the balcony, at the top of our castle. We waved to the people below.

Sounds of *oooh* and *ahhh* came from the crowd. Maura headed to her right, and I headed left. We both boarded the elevators we had previously called to the top floor, came down to the bottom floor, and met at the top of the stairs. We grasped each other's hands and walked down the stairs to take our place as the happy couple, while our arrival music continued to play.

Our preacher was our dear friend, Benjamin, the one who had introduced us. He was an ordained minister, so he was able to marry us. Maura had created a stress-free day, as she had proclaimed it would be. Everything about this wedding was perfect.

We had flown Timar in for the wedding, and he was our ring bearer, also dressed in Renaissance costume like Maura and me. He was so cute.

My dear friend, Jamie Green, sang "You Are So Beautiful to Me," popularized by Joe Cocker. Maura and I stood together and performed expressive Sufi hand movements during a song called "Use Me," by Rickie Byars Beckwith and Reverend Michael Beckwith.

Our ceremony was short but sweet. We did the hug line and moved into the restaurant to feast like a prince and princess should. It was incredible to have so many people we loved all together. Some people from my family whom I had not seen in years were there. Even my father had flown in for the wedding. He was sitting across from my mother at one of the tables. When I noticed, my eyes started to water.

Maura asked me, "What's going on?"

I answered, "I can honestly not remember my parents ever sitting at the same table together, or even getting along well in the same room. This is just so amazing."

The food was spectacular, and the guests had a great time. Maura and I were more interested in visiting with people at the reception than we were in eating. We managed to get a bite of food in now and then. The owners had created a sweet little tiramisu cake for us to cut, with the guests to be served their own individual serving after we had completed this wedding ritual.

Maura and I had decided that we were not going to smash cake in each other's face. As much as the crowd egged us on, we would not do it.

I said, "You know, all the people who smoosh the cake in each other's faces at their wedding are divorced now. Think about it."

The crowd responded with a laugh, as they realized there was truth to what I had just said.

After we had feasted, we went outside, where all the chairs had been removed to create a place for dancing. Our dance was first. Maura and I looked each other in the eyes and cried with joy as we danced to the song, "Love Will Come to You," by the Indigo Girls. Next, we did the traditional father-daughter and mother-son dances, and then we did the dollar dance, which was great fun.

After the traditional dances were over, we all danced together to songs I had chosen. My dad was cutting a rug thanks to having recovered fully from a recent knee replacement operation. My older sister danced with me, reminding us of when she taught me how to dance when I was a child. Before we knew it, people started to head home and the wedding was over.

It was exactly what Maura—and I—had envisioned: a beautiful, stress-free event—one that nobody would soon forget.

Part IV

The Path to Living My Purpose

12

More Lessons, More Setbacks

After the Wedding Bliss

I wish I could say that, after the wedding, everything went smoothly, and I was immediately able to live my life's purpose, but there was still some more work to do.

I had come to know, with the help of my angels, that I was here to touch and inspire the lives of those with whom I came into contact.

I was now aware that my purpose involved speaking, teaching, singing, writing, and publishing.

But, good things take time, and there were more lessons to be learned.

Although I had a great relationship with the owners of Face Broadcast Productions, I found myself wanting to move on. More and more, I wanted to work for myself. I had a dream of opening up my own production company. Maura agreed, so I put in my notice and left my position just before we got married. Ron and Jamie were sad I was leaving, but there were no hard feelings. Of course, we invited them to come to our wedding, and they attended together.

We spent our honeymoon in a cozy cabin in the mountains of Southern California. Remember, I had always dreamed of having a home in the mountains, so this was a perfect spot for us to spend our honeymoon.

When we returned from our honeymoon, I contacted my best friend Rudy. I reminded him how we had always dreamed of starting our own production company. It didn't take much coercing, and before you knew it, Rudy put in his notice at Face. We started planning our own video production business. We had plenty of connections to producers we had met over the years at Face. We didn't take any business from them, merely asked for referrals to people they knew who could use our services.

It took a little while to get the business up and going, but by September of that year, our new business, Wizard Vision Productions was doing quite well.

New Struggles Begin

Then, on September 11, 2001, early in the morning, the phone rang, waking Maura and me up.

"Hello," I said, with a gravelly, just-opened-up-my-eyes kind of voice. It was Rudy on the phone.

"Turn on the TV."

"Oh my God, what is that?"

"Someone just bombed the twin towers in New York. It's horrible."

"I've got to go, Rudy; I'll call you back later."

Maura and I sat in silence as we watched this story unfold. Time passed and then another plane flew into the side of the second building. It just kept getting worse as the day went on.

After this day, this event continued to rock the nation. America was completely consumed with this story—and rightly so. All cameras headed immediately to New York, and film production effectively came to a halt, dramatically affecting our business.

Before Rudy and I knew it, there was no work to be found for us. Even the big, well-established production houses were taking a major hit, so people like Rudy and I found ourselves with nothing.

Rudy had created his own list, and had manifested a girlfriend of his own that was his perfect match. She asked him to move in with her, and he agreed. His new place was over an hour away. With the lack of business and this costly and inconvenient commute, I decided I would stop working with Rudy and look for a job.

I wasn't anticipating a problem.

I had never had a problem getting a job before; why would this be any different?

It was. I searched and searched and could not find a job. I had the perfect resume and I interviewed well. I pulled out all the stops and employed every trick that had gotten me jobs in the past. Nothing worked.

Maura was waitressing part-time at a restaurant, and somehow, up to this point, we were making it work. We had some money that I had put away when I was working at Face, and we had some wedding gifts that were helping, but our savings were disappearing quickly.

Maura and I attended a weeklong seminar retreat together. Much of the retreat involved silent meditation, which left me alone with my thoughts—not a great place to be at this point. We were just about to run out of money except for what Maura was earning at the restaurant. My son was now living with us, and I needed to provide for him.

I kept coming back to one thought: *Welfare.*

The word evoked a kind of horror for me. I've told you the history of my childhood. You remember that, because of my mom's circumstances, I was a welfare child. I had sworn that I would never ever go on welfare myself.

This thought kept recurring as I pondered during the silence.

At this retreat, I met a man who had done very well for himself in business. He was well off and experienced—he had lived it all and seen it all. During the retreat, he became a mentor for me. At one of the times when we could talk during the retreat, I informed the man of the situation and asked his advice.

He didn't beat around the bush.

He said, bluntly, "You have to put your ego aside, my friend. Your child is far more important than your little ego. You must provide for him and that means, no matter what you have to do, you must make sure he has a roof over his head, clothes on his back, and food in his stomach. Promise me that the day after we return to the land of the living, you will go and apply for welfare. Promise me."

"I promise."

"Good for you, Keith. That's a decision made by a good father right there. That's what it looks like."

Upon our return, I did go and apply for welfare, and I got it. It wasn't a lot, but combined with the money Maura was making as a waitress, we were able to squeak by—just barely. I continued my job search to no avail.

The welfare program required me to go to a career center on a daily basis. On my first visit, I was assigned to a counselor. She and I connected, and the first thing she asked me to do was to go work on my resume. I thought I already had a good resume, but using their system, I decided to update it, shift a few things around, and work on the overall look of it. I checked in with her after I had completed it, and she approved.

I followed the requirements diligently. There was a repetitive schedule. First, I came in to the career center, checked the want ads, and made interview appointments. The next day, I went out looking for a job, and the following day, returned to the career center, jobless. At that point, the cycle repeated.

I met with the counselor again, and we discussed how I was interviewing. The counselor did a mock interview with me and quickly understood that I was different than most of the people she had worked with. I had already had much success in my life, and had never had a problem getting a job before. She began to entertain the idea that perhaps there just weren't any jobs out there for me in that moment.

The Job Search Continues; a New Project Begins

Maura and I had started talking about writing a book. We had a great marriage and people around us had noticed how well we communicated with each other. In fact, so many people had asked us about the communication tool we were using that we became interested, ourselves, in the process that we used. We started to dissect it.

Once, when we had an argument, Maura paused and said, "Do you mind if I go get a pencil and some paper?"

We stopped and wrote down the entire argument, which included the way we were communicating. In the end, we discovered that we had created a tool we now call *The Format*.

My counselor encouraged the book writing process. Maybe she was just placating me at the time, thinking I was just talking and would never actually do the writing. Maura and I, however, were taking this endeavor seriously.

We actively went to work writing the book. I brought in a few of the working chapters, and saw my counselor's expression change as she read. By the time she finished, she had the look of a proud mama on her face!

We were happy to be working on the book, but still needed money. As of yet, I had not found a job. I continued to look regularly and still could find nothing.

I was at the end of my rope. To put it plainly, I was feeling like a loser. I felt like I had let my wife and my son down. I felt like I had let myself down. To top it off, I was still on welfare, which continued to push those degrading buttons in my psyche. I was constantly battling feelings of shame.

I was getting close to giving up when the phone rang. It was my friend, Rudy.

He said, "My girlfriend wants to talk to you. You have restaurant experience right?"

I confirmed this and she got on the line. She asked what kind of experience I had.

"I've been a busboy, a waiter, a bar manager, and I am a well-trained show bartender. I'm a great bartender, as a matter-of-fact."

His girlfriend's name was Nida, and she worked in personnel for a large hotel company. She explained that they had an Embassy Suites Hotel near LAX, and she would check with the general manager to see what job openings they had.

She said, "I may be able to get you in over there. Go to the restaurant and tell the restaurant manager I sent you. You'll get an interview."

"Thank you, thank you so much. Who should I ask for when I call?"

She told me that the restaurant manager's name was Brian and that I should tell him that Nida, the manager from human resources at corporate, had sent me.

"I will. I'll do that right away. I really appreciate it."

I immediately called the hotel and asked for Brian. He and I worked out a time the next day when I would come and meet with him. I called my counselor at the career center and told her I had an interview. She was excited for me.

The next day, I showed up at the hotel restaurant and asked for Brian. I interviewed with him, and he said he would get back to me. When I followed up a few days later, he told me that they weren't looking to fill that position just yet, and I should check back at a later date.

I called Nida and told her what he had said. Nida wasted no time before responding.

She called the hotel's general manager. Later, she told me that she said, "I sent my friend Keith there to interview with Brian. He's qualified but Brian is putting him off."

The hotel manager said to her, "Brian is not sure if Keith is a good fit. He's still thinking about it."

Nida got testy then.

She said to him, "I'm not sure what part of *hire my friend* you folks don't understand down there. He is qualified, and you will be glad you hired him; he will be one of the best employees you'll ever have. I'm asking you—hire him; you won't regret it."

Nida called me back and told me, "Call Brian tomorrow and I think he will have a more favorable response for you. I had to put my foot down a bit, but I'm pretty sure they will find a spot for you on the schedule.

I thanked her and told her, "This means the world to me, Nida. It was getting ugly inside my head, and I was just about to give up on myself. I really appreciate your help."

"Don't worry about it, Keith. Just be the best employee they've ever had so I can rub it in that manager's face."

I laughed and said, "You got it. Will do."

By the way, in addition to being the personnel manager of the hotel company, Nida was also an etheric healer and is someone I have come to know as being very connected to the angelic realm. In retrospect, it's no surprise that she would contact me the moment I was about to give up on myself.

The next day when I contacted Brian, he miraculously did have room on the schedule for me. However, it had been true that they didn't have a spot open for a bartender, so I started as a waiter. It was a pleasure to call my career counselor and tell her I had gotten a job. She congratulated me and told me she couldn't wait to read the book we were writing.

I hadn't waited tables in a while, so I was a bit out of practice. Maura, however, was one of the best waitresses I knew, and she was able to give me many tips, for which I was grateful. It was one hell of a drive from where I lived to LAX, but it wasn't long before Maura left her job so we could move closer. Our new place was also closer to our spiritual center, Agape.

Embassy Suites had another position available, so I suggested she apply. One thing that's cool about the hotel industry is that it's a family affair.

There were many family members working together at this hotel. The wife of the executive chef was the head of housekeeping. There were tons of brothers and sisters working in housekeeping. They wouldn't have a problem with a husband and wife team on the serving staff. I made an appointment for Maura to interview with the manager.

The interview was a funny experience—both for Maura and for the manager, I think.

She was completely indifferent regarding this job and was, quite frankly, just going through the motions. To her, it was just a way to make a little more money while we were working on our book. She knew she was more than qualified for the job, and they would be lucky to get her to work for them.

Maura said the manager was so serious with his questions that it was like being interviewed for a corporate management job. Maura is honest, straightforward, and a bit of a character; that manager never knew what hit him.

To give you an idea of how it went; during the course of the interview, he asked her, "Where do you see yourself in five years?"

"Certainly not here," Maura replied.

See what I mean?

During the interview, her poise impressed him so much that, before she knew it, he was offering her a job as assistant manager, working under him.

She respectfully declined and said she was perfectly happy to be a waitress. It was a lot less stress, and the hours would be more flexible, which was what she was looking for. She told him that, after all, she and her husband were writing a book that was sure to be a bestseller—it wouldn't be long before they would be on Oprah—and the plan was only to work there until all that happened. He admired her decision, tried a little more to talk her out of it, but eventually put her on the schedule as a waitress.

It wasn't more than a few months before I was asked to fill an empty slot as a bartender. Together, we made enough money to cover all our bills, and we continued to work at that hotel as we finished writing our book.

We met many new people at our workplace, both co-workers and guests. Maura and I noticed that the conversations largely consisted of mutual complaints.

It is a common situation, as you may know from personal experience. The conversations around the water cooler are not usually positive and constructive.

At this hotel, we heard:

"Mucho trabajo, poco dinero."

"I'm already working so much but I think I'm going to have to get a third job. Life is so rough."

"Did you see the news last night? Life is so horrible."

During this time, Maura and I had obtained a CD series by Terry Cole-Whittaker, the queen of positive affirmations. We created a daily ritual of repeating the affirmations—statements purposefully designed to create what you want in life.

Maura and I became walking, talking affirmations.

How did people react to us?

Honestly, people thought we were weirdos, but they loved us. We made them feel good. Even the corporate guests at the hotel reacted positively to our conversations.

We told them things like:

"Everything is going to be all right. You are awesome. You can do anything you put your mind to. Don't get used to seeing us around here—we are going to have a huge best-selling book, and go on Oprah. Life is good, isn't it?"

We were both making decent money then, enjoying the flexibility of the hours. However, it was taking a toll on our bodies. After all, we were not twenty-somethings anymore. I was forty years old and my son was in high school. Maura was just about to turn forty herself, and we were beginning to feel our age.

Time was flying by.

The Seven Steps Book Launch (2005)

Once we finished writing our book, *The Seven Steps to Successful Relationships,* we got our friend, Rudy, to do the layout. Rudy's mother was a well-known spiritual leader who had written several books. Rudy had not only created the covers for those books, but he had done the layout as well.

Next, we needed enough money to complete the production phase, which included the book cover, ISBN number, and the printing of the books.

We decided the best way to do this would be to have a fundraiser dinner at the hotel where we worked. They had banquets there regularly, and I was good friends with the banquet manager. He arranged a special price for us for the rental of the room and a great price per plate for our guests. We booked it and invited everyone we knew. We invited friends, family members, hotel employees, people we knew from church—anyone we could think of.

The turnout was huge, and the event was amazing. Lots of friends and family showed up and it was a great night. Maura and I did a comedy routine about how we used to communicate. People about fell off their chairs, they were laughing so hard. Our friends were surprised to find out that we could do comedy together so well—and so were Maura and I.

I played some music and invited a few of the employees to perform with me. We danced and partied into the night. The event was a smashing success. We raised enough money to pay for the room and the food, to get the book cover done, and to print a few hundred books, including shipping fees.

The highlight of the evening for me was my older sister pulling me aside to tell me how proud she was of me. It wasn't long after this night that she passed away, and I am grateful to have that moment forever in my memory.

Receiving our books in the mail was exciting. Before long, there were tons of boxes stacked all over the house. We were finally published authors, and it felt great.

However, I had no idea how to sell the books.

We hadn't planned that part. We had tracked down the number one author in relationship books, John Gray, and had secured his endorsement for the front cover of our book. After that, I think that we just thought the rest would take care of itself—the books would just be flying off the shelves.

So, to summarize, there were two problems:

How do we get our books on the shelves in the first place?

How do we market them once we get them out there?

I hadn't thought that far ahead and didn't know the first thing about answering either of these questions. I had no idea that this book would become my credibility, and my business card, and that it was our steppingstone to bigger stages of progress in our lives.

All I had were boxes of books doubling for end tables and posing as a coffee table.

What is *The Secret*?

Shortly after our book came out, we received an e-mail that contained a link to the trailer for a new movie that Reverend Michael Beckwith, from Agape, was featured in. The trailer was hot, and we couldn't wait for this movie, called *The Secret,* to come out. We thought the campaign for this movie—a viral on-line campaign—was a stroke of genius.

The movie was all about the law of attraction. You will remember that the law of attraction is what my friend Rudy had taught me about years before. It was what Maura and I had used to attract each other. We had known about the law of attraction for years, and now the world would know about it. *The Secret* was a smash—it is now referred to as *The Secret Phenomenon.*

It was an incredibly motivational movie. When we finished watching it, I looked at Maura. I talked to her about the teachers who had been featured in the movie.

I said, "I really like those people. They inspire me. I don't want to just meet them, I want to work with them, I want to do business with them, I want to be friends with them, and I want to break bread with them."

I had spoken the word and ordered it from the universe, and soon, it came to be.

Because Reverend Michael had worked with them in the movie, one by one, those teachers showed up to speak at Agape. One by one, I was able to meet them, spend time with them, and do business with them, just as I had ordered.

While we continued to work at the hotel and perform affirmations daily, we were exploring the world of online communication. I was on a social media network called MySpace and Maura had become active in an online chat room/forum that interested her.

In my online group, called *Committed to Love,* I dispensed relationship advice. I was helping people attract their perfect mates—using *The List* technique—as well as helping many people with their current relationships.

In Maura's forum, there were heated conversations going back and forth. Maura served as a peacekeeper in that forum. Someone from the company, who had become aware of what Maura was doing so eloquently, asked her if she would be a volunteer forum moderator. She obliged. She did such a great job that they ultimately offered her a contract position with the company.

We now had our first client. We had started our own business, and now had a paying client. Maura and I celebrated the moment. We knew that, in the near future, we would be leaving our restaurant jobs.

And so it came to be!

It wasn't long before the online job replaced Maura's income, so she put in her notice at the hotel. Soon, the company Maura was working with approached us with a proposal. They knew that we had written a book together and that we were a dynamic team. They contracted with the two of us to be their corporate trainers.

With the new income this contract brought, I was also able to quit working at the hotel. It was the last job I would ever have working for someone else. We have been blessed enough to have been the owners of our own business ever since, and we've never looked back.

One Million Love Notes

Maura and I were asked to train our new client's sales force. We had also been working on finding effective ways to acquire our own individual clients to coach, but were having a tough time figuring out how to do this. We didn't know it, but the key was in those stacks of books, collecting dust in our garage.

We continued to work as trainers for this company until we were notified that they were going out of business.

Soon, we had lost the client that had been the source of all our income. Thankfully, it wasn't long before we landed a contract as coaches for one of the largest seminar training companies in the world. Before we knew it, I had thirty-five coaching clients and Maura had thirty-two.

Meanwhile, we were knee-deep in a campaign called *One Million Love Notes*. We had an idea that would help us raise money for our favorite organization, EDUCARE, that worked with teenagers. We would be able to raise money for them and, at the same time, have a successful campaign that would surely shine a light on our company. While we worked full-time as coaches, we worked the other hours to do whatever we could to make the One Million Love Notes project a success.

The day of the big launch was Valentine's Day, 2006. We were excited to begin the day, but in the end, we sold only 156 love notes. Talk about a letdown. We were extremely disappointed. It felt like our biggest failure to date. Maura was devastated. She said she wanted to take some time off from our business and just coach for the seminar organization for a while.

I looked at Maura and said, "Sure, I'm glad to take over our business, I just need the best book title I've ever heard and then, I'll be off and running."

Who Do You Think You Are?

Maura has a gift. She can come up with great book titles and subtitles all day long.

After I said, "I just need the best book title I've ever heard and I'll be off and running," it took her all about a minute and a half to look at me and say, "Who do you think you are?"

I said, "What, what did I do?"

"No, silly, that's the book title: *Who Do You Think You Are?*"

"Oh."

She continued, "Get it? It grabs your attention because most people have a negative view of that question, like you just demonstrated."

She was right, of course.

"Now, come up with an idea for the book, and a great subtitle, and you are in business."

I was blown away. This was the best book title I had ever heard.

I started to ponder: *What would the book be about? What did I want to write? What would be appropriate content for this amazing title:* Who Do You Think You Are?

First, I thought it could be a book about millionaires. I could interview millionaires and ask them who they think they are, what series of events happened to create their millions, and what advice would they give to people who wanted to be rich.

I reached out to one of the featured teachers from the movie, *The Secret,* and asked him to take a meeting with me. He said he was flying into the country the next week. I could pick him up at the airport, take him to his hotel, and we could have a meeting.

I went to Maura and said, "I have a meeting booked with one of the teachers from *The Secret*.

"A meeting about what?"

"About my book."

She was mystified.

"Which book would that be?"

"Who Do You Think You Are?"

"That book idea is half-baked."

"Well, we'd better bake it quickly because I have a meeting with this guy next week. We're picking him up at LAX, taking him to his hotel and then we have a lunch meeting scheduled to discuss the possibility of him co-authoring the book with me."

Maura raised her eyebrows and grinned. I think she was already seeing the difference between how *we* ran the company, and how it was going to be now that *I* was running it.

We met the man at LAX, and it was amazing. He taught me so much, and he even agreed to co-author the book with me. Not long after this meeting, I realized that this book idea about millionaires fit Maura's title very well, but writing it didn't seem like a good fit for me. I would want to add my own story to any book I worked on, and at this point, I certainly wasn't a millionaire.

What would I be able to add to a book about becoming one?

The next day, I sat in meditation and focused on the title: *Who Do You Think You Are?*

I asked the question: *What will this book be about?*

The movie in my mind started up, and it showed me in my early twenties when I was in Fresno. I was on a search to discover my purpose. I had gone to every church, synagogue, and mosque, searching. If there was someone in the park standing on a box preaching, I was there. No one had the answer for me, and I hadn't sensed God in any of the places of worship.

I had wished, at that time, that I could sit down and pick the brains of all the people I felt were living their purpose in life. I wished I could ask them all questions about how they made their discoveries, and find out what they recommended for me as a young man on my own search.

As I watched the movie in my mind, I realized that many of the people I had wished I could have talked with in my youth, I now knew personally. I was also filled with gratitude that I had finally learned my purpose, with help from my angels.

Finally, I understood what I should write about.

You see it, right?

The book would be: *Who Do You Think You Are? Discover the Purpose of Your Life.*

It just came to me, as if it had been absorbed from the air around me. To use a computer metaphor, it felt like this idea had been downloaded from the angels into my mind. I took a minute to breathe it in, and it felt right. This idea was juicy and exciting.

I would interview people who were actively living their purpose and write about them. I would be writing to help the people who were still searching for their purpose. Just the thought of it was stirring me inside in a good way. This time, I had something personal to offer to this book—my own story. It felt right. I decided I was on track and ready to begin.

On the Advice of Angels

I asked my angels: *What are my next steps?*

As usual, I heard a voice in response. It told me to create a list of all the people I felt were truly living their purpose in life. I was told not to limit myself in any way. If they were famous, put them down anyway. Not even the sky was a limit on this one. I opened my eyes, took a breath, and started to create my list.

I started with the people I already knew. Next, I wrote down the authors of books that had changed my life. I wrote down people whose seminars I had attended and experienced transformation. Next, I thought about celebrities that were obviously living their purpose. I continued to write every name that came to me, without editing, and the next thing I knew, I was staring at a list of eighty people. I looked up and realized it was time for my first coaching call of the day.

At the end of the coaching day, I filled Maura in about my progress. She quickly helped me dial in the three questions I would ask the book participants.

The three questions would be:

1. *Who Do You Think You Are?* For the people we interviewed, we knew we would need to explain what this meant. We would ask them: *Why are you here? What is your purpose in life?*
2. *What event, or series of events, led to the discovery of your purpose?*
3. *If you could give advice to those who are searching for their purpose in life, what would it be?*

The next day, I sat looking at my list and got even more excited as I read the names of these remarkable people.

I remember thinking: *If I even get half of these people, this will be the best book ever.*

This list included Bob Proctor, John Gray, Marci Shimoff, John Demartini, John Assaraf, Joe Vitale, and more. Ten people from the movie *The Secret* were on the list. It was going to feature musicians, doctors, entrepreneurs, teachers, and best-selling authors. Of course, I had no idea how I was going to reach the people on my list.

I decided to consult my angels once again.

I closed my eyes, and took the breath of life while focusing on the question: *How will I contact these people?*

I continued to breathe and ask the question. Nothing. I continued to breathe and ask the question. Still nothing. I kept breathing until, like a flash, an instant download of a complete process came to me. I quickly opened up my eyes and wrote it down. I call it *the elevator email,* and I now teach it to my writing students as a regular part of my course.

Are you familiar with the *elevator speech* tactic?

Using this common tactic, you would devise a short speech—shorter than an average elevator ride—that could convince someone to support you or a project you're working on. You would consider what you would say if you were riding in an elevator with someone who could help you with a problem, knowing you had to finish your speech during that shared elevator ride. It is a useful technique for designing some types of sales pitches.

My *elevator email* is like an elevator speech, only in email form, and it has been remarkably useful for me and for my students.

In the past, I had a fear of using the phone for marketing, and this fear had made me unable to use phone calls effectively for business. A specific process the angels gave me was, ultimately, what got me over my fear.

This is how it worked: I put up copies of all the books of my friends, mentors, and favorite authors I wanted in the book, with their photos facing me, and I used them to coerce myself into calling them.

I looked at each of their photos and, in my head, I imagined each of them saying things like, "Call me, Keith—you can do this—call me up—you have a great project, of course I will say yes—pick up the phone, Keith—you've got this!"

For the first few calls, my heart was pounding so hard I could feel it in my neck, but after getting some *yes* answers from people, I relaxed into it and got over my fear.

Using the advice of my angels turned out to be very successful. Of my list of eighty people, I ended up getting sixty-eight yes answers using the processes the angels had given me once I meditated on the right questions.

As I worked on planning and writing this book, I developed a routine. Every morning, I sat down, cleared out any notion of what I thought I had to do that day, and asked questions of my angels, then waited for the answers.

If I didn't have a question for the day, I would ask: *What am I to do next? What is my next step?*

This new way of being was creating wonderfully successful outcomes.

The difference between how Maura and I had done business previously, and the way I was doing it now, was becoming obvious. When faced with decisions before, Maura and I always thought we knew what to do, and we just set out to do it. Maura was an over-thinker. Every step was thought out, discussed, and planned down to the last detail.

What's wrong with this structure?

Nothing, but we'd had no success working that way.

Now, I sat down every morning and cleared out any notion of what I thought I had to do that day. I would ask clear questions, and then, I would wait for the answers. This new way of being was working much better than our old method.

One day in meditation, I was informed that I should ask Jack Canfield if he would co-author the book with me. That was an exciting meditation outcome for sure. He was co-author of a book that changed my life forever. Now, perhaps he would co-author a book with me.

Using a specific format given to me by my angels (I now call *right asking*) for reaching out to people of influence, I contacted Jack Canfield's office. I set up an interview to ask him the three questions, and by the end of our call, he had agreed to do the book with me. Jack reached out to his publisher, HarperCollins. They reminded Jack that he had several books in line before mine and gave us a targeted release date that was four to six years out.

I didn't have any interest in a date that far into the future. Our book would feature ten mentors from *The Secret*. We intended to springboard off the success and momentum that the movie had created, so we couldn't wait.

Next, we presented *Who Do You Think You Are?* to the publishers of the *Chicken Soup for the Soul Series®* but they wanted to turn it into a Chicken Soup book, which involved a name change.

I had no interest in a name change. The name had everything to do with the book subject, and that had been divinely downloaded from source and angels. After consulting some of the other teachers from *The Secret* who I knew had created bestsellers themselves, I decided to self-publish the book and go it alone.

I told Jack and he said, "Let me know what would you like me to do, Keith and I'll do it."

I asked him if he would write the foreword and support the book when it released. He kindly agreed.

I did most of the book interviews over the phone and recorded them in an online conference room in between my coaching calls. Remember, I still had thirty-five coaching clients from the seminar company. I was booked solid, six days a week. I rested only on Sunday when I attended Agape and enjoyed the rest of the day at the beach, snuggling with Maura, or connecting with Agape folks.

13

Two Steps Forward, One Step Back

As I neared the end of the interview process, I still hadn't figured out what to do about publishing, and hadn't decided how I would launch the book. My first book hadn't been the best seller I'd envisioned, so I wanted to be sure to choose wisely this time. When I sat down in meditation pondering these questions, it became clear to me that I should reach out and ask the advice of the teachers I had interviewed—those who had created massive bestsellers of their own.

The first person I spoke to was Joe Vitale, a featured teacher from *The Secret*. He encouraged me to self-publish. Since I'd done all the work, I should get all the money. Then he pointed out two important factors. One, I wasn't publishing this book to make money but to change lives. Approaching the process from this place would be authentic and would make a huge difference. Second, everyone I had interviewed had email lists of followers and fans. The teachers from *The Secret* alone probably had over a million names combined. I would work with the contributors to create a series of emails to be launched with the book's release.

I also took some time to get support and mentorship from other contributors who had successful books. I received help everywhere I asked, demonstrating a principle that I have been shown many times—*doers like helping doers.*

At this point, I knew all the steps I needed to take, but it was necessary to put them in the right order, with the right timing. Once again, I received what I needed in the form of a new contact.

A Meeting Made in Heaven

Not long after this, I was speaking at an event in Los Angeles. I told another speaker that I had all the elements of a joint venture book launch, but I didn't know how to put them into order. Without hesitation, this person immediately referred me to Gina Romanello. I called her, and we arranged for a meeting at a restaurant in Long Beach. It would later became apparent that we had been divinely guided to each other.

After introductions, she said, "Tell me your story. What's the book about and how did you get to where we are today?"

I told her my story, and we soon realized why we had been brought together. We had been following closely aligned paths for years. She'd organized book launches for Jack Canfield and many others I had met and admired. She had done the launch for the exact Jack Canfield book I had used as my model for *Who Do You Think You Are?* The book was titled, *You've Got to Read This Book.* I loved the book so much I had used it as a model to guide my journey for my book.

We sat and talked for ninety minutes more, building a great connection. When Gina had to leave to get to another meeting, we set a date to meet a few days later. She told me to bring my detailed list of steps, and she would help me sort it all out. That is exactly what she did. She reviewed all the steps I had written, took them home, and created a tool that I still use. It is now included in my home study course: *Bake Your Book Bestseller Campaign Roadmap*™.

Gina was tremendously instrumental in the joint venture campaign for *Who Do You Think You Are?* With her guidance and support, we established an appropriate and strategically ordered timeline for the publication process. It isn't overstating to say that she was the final piece of the puzzle that changed my life forever. She has also become a dear friend.

With the roadmap to a successful joint venture campaign in place, focus shifted to implementation. We obtained quotes for everything we couldn't do ourselves and found out we needed a lot more money than we had. I contacted a few friends and clients with a great offer. They would lend us the money for an agreed amount of time and receive a very nice interest rate in return. Because I had the support of so many successful people and a cutting-edge marketing plan, it didn't take long to raise the money needed.

Somehow, by the grace of God, and with the help of a band of angels, we rolled out a full-scale joint venture campaign. It was truly an amazing feat. Looking back, I'm not sure how Maura and I pulled off something that should have required a six- to eight-person team, but we did. The webpages were beautiful, the bonuses were juicy, and the names associated with the project were big. We were set to launch in April 2008.

Over 1.5 million emails went out the morning of the launch. We set it up so we would receive an email every time a sale was made. For days, our email box dinged like a winning Vegas slot machine. This was like nothing we had experienced in our business lives so far.

Even elements outside our control supported our goals. A few weeks prior to our launch, Oprah had Eckhart Tolle on her show with his book, *A New Earth: Awakening to Your Life's Purpose*.

Friends were afraid this would distract from our book, but Maura and I knew we had just been given an incredible gift: *Oprah had just made finding your life's purpose the number one topic of conversation in America.*

We ended up on the front page in the bestsellers section on Amazon, right underneath Tolle's book. Our book was listed under Amazon's recommendation heading: *If you like that book, you'll also like this.* The timing couldn't have been better.

Who Do You Think You Are? became a bestseller just a few hours after it was launched, and stayed on the list for weeks.

As a bonus, many people who discovered our life purpose book also went on to purchase our first book, *The Seven Steps to Successful Relationships.* As a result, it would become a bestseller in several categories.

When You Least Expect It, Expect It.

We were a few days into this wonderful launch, and Maura and I were basking in the excitement of our success, when we received a call. My mother had fallen and wasn't doing well. We immediately went to her house.

My mother hadn't been taking good care of herself, and at the house, we found her issues as a hoarder evident everywhere. After some deep conversations with her, we determined that she could no longer be responsible for herself. After much begging and pleading from her, we decided we had no other choice but to take her out of the house.

With her plaintive cry, "Please, don't put me in a home," ringing in our ears, we searched for a facility that would suit her needs.

We found a place for my mother in my hometown. It was a full-care facility and appeared to be a good one. A few days later, we moved her there and went to work on clearing out her apartment.

I rented a storage unit where we would put the things we decided to keep. Sorting through the mess brought back many memories, mostly unpleasant, of my youth. She had accumulated so much that, even after a week of cleaning, I had barely made a dent.

I was fascinated to discover that she had made some plans for this process; she had hidden notes for me all through the house.

Son-shine, you mean the world to me.

I have always loved you, Son-shine.

Thanks for all you did for me and for the boys.

The notes were heartbreaking to read. All they did was remind me of her deteriorating health.

I kept thinking: *What if she had already died when I was discovering these notes?*

It didn't take me long to realize I was sorting through four generations of memories. As I picked up one object after another, I was feeling the energy and the pain of this manic-depressive woman at different ages. I could see the anguish in all their eyes as I sifted through photos, books, jewelry, paintings, and more, trying to decide what to keep and what to toss.

I was managing pretty well until I found a series of boxes belonging to my sister, who had died the previous year of an accidental overdose.

A wave of grief unlike any I had ever experienced before came over me, and things began to go black. Maura found me that way and quickly got my nephew on the phone. I spoke to him, and then Maura caught him up on what was happening.

He came over as soon as he could. It took Maura, my nephew, and me, along with a small army of rotating friends, almost a whole month to sort, dump, and pack. This was one of the most painful and laborious tasks I had ever endured. Afterwards, I was exhausted, physically and emotionally.

I felt overwhelmed by guilt from two directions.

First, I had just put my mother in a home, which I had said I'd never do, and second, I felt like I was letting Maura down just as we were having some financial and professional success.

My mother needed our support and care, however, and she needed help adjusting to her new living situation. There was nobody else who could take care of her. We decided to move back to my hometown where we would find a smaller place close to mom.

Once again, I was back to juggling a month-to-month schedule, trying to manage all the elements of our lives.

14

Changing Directions and the Birth of the Book Guy

Unfortunately, taking care of my mother meant the momentum we had built for the launch came to a screeching halt. I had to cancel radio interviews, tele-seminars, and speaking engagements so I could look after my mother's affairs.

I continued to seek support and advice from some of my new mentors. A new concept I learned during this time was to start thinking of the book I had just published as my business card.

A book as a business card?

If that sounds strange to you, I don't blame you a bit.

Think about the purpose of a business card. When you give someone your business card, you are giving that person something to help them remember you. In addition, your card contains your contact information so they can to get in touch with you. Often, a card contains a logo, the name of your business, and maybe, a motto.

If, instead, you give them a book that you wrote, you are giving them an object that contains all this information—usually conveniently found at the end of the book—plus a great deal of additional detail about you. In addition, it gives them the evidence that you have the skill and the focus to *write a book*—and that says something truly special about you.

Using a book in this way would help give me new credibility, which, if used correctly, would help me to gain clients. Even more important, it could get me onto a bigger stage from which I could reach even more people.

I started using my book as my business card from that point forward. It had already helped me to secure several interviews that were helpful for promotion of my business. I wrote up a speaker proposal and started looking for speaking gigs. Being a best-selling author opened doors to being a featured speaker on much larger stages, as well as on tele-seminars and webinars. My book helped me to become featured in programs—some of them hosted by teachers from my book—and gain my own book mentor clients. In addition, I was fielding invitations to take part in other joint venture book campaigns. My book was a launch pad to success.

I was often invited to speak at events that were focused on life purpose, but the strangest thing kept happening to me. Even though I was speaking about life purpose, and talking about my book on the subject, people kept calling me *The Book Guy*.

Yes, I Am the Book Guy

When I would speak, I'd begin by telling everyone how I got to be on the stage before them. My story always included the creation of *Who Do You Think You Are*, letting the listeners know that it went from idea to best-selling book in less than a year.

No matter what else I spoke about at the event, afterwards, people would come up to me to talk about the writing of the book.

I was constantly hearing:

"You're the book guy, right? I want to talk to you about doing a book"

"Do you teach how to get interviews with people for a book?"

After hearing these questions about two dozen times, I looked up to the heavens and said: *Okay, I get it God.*

The people had spoken, and they had pointed me toward my next step.

I checked an internet registration site for the domain name *TheyCallMeTheBookGuy.com* and it was available.

I went to prayer and meditation with it, and I soon realized that being *The Book Guy* was an integral part of my purpose. My angels had guided me to write my book about life purpose, and, in doing so, had brought me to a new realization.

In meditation, I realized that, in the process of living my purpose, I had learned something that inspired others. It would have taken me over ten years, and well over a hundred thousand dollars, to gain the education I had amassed in a nine-month period. It became clear to me that it was my responsibility to teach authors and entrepreneurs how to write and market their books. The angels had shown me another part of my life purpose.

I made the transition slowly and started offering personal book mentor packages as part of my live seminar offering. Since I needed to work with people one at a time, I scheduled only small groups for book mentoring. Working with a larger group felt too daunting, and Maura couldn't assist much because she was coaching full-time.

We were also donating our time as coaches at an event called *Life Directions,* hosted by the seminar company. Working for this company had afforded us the luxury of creating our book campaign, and volunteering at this annual event was our way of giving back.

We were there to coach the students, to help them to discover their purpose or their life direction, and to answer any questions they had at the event. We were not there to sell anything, just to be of service in any way we could. People were lined up to work with us—it was like a coaching marathon.

Bake Your Book

On the last day of the event, I met Maribel Jimenez. She was a marketing expert who approached me with an interesting proposal. She wanted to help me find a way to create a group-mentoring program that wouldn't be overwhelming for us to manage. We agreed to speak over the phone one afternoon after the event.

Not only was I interested in hearing her ideas about creating a group mentoring program, I was also interested in finding out where she learned the exact way she had asked me for this appointment. One of the skills I have been teaching was a skill called *right asking* and this young woman had performed this process perfectly, even using some of the exact language I use when I teach the technique.

Maribel began by telling me about her life and business experience.

After a short time, I asked her, "You know the way you asked me for this meeting? Where did you learn that?

She explained, "A while ago, I was part of a Golden Circle program with a well-known married couple, and part of the program included teaching calls with well-known experts. The experts would teach us ways to take our business to the next level. One of these experts, a multiple best-selling author, taught us a skill called *right asking*—"

She broke off after she said these words, and paused for a few seconds.

She took a breath and said, "Oh, my God, you are the one who teaches that, aren't you? It was you on that call, right?"

I smiled, "Yes, yes it was. I recognized the technique when you stepped up and *right-asked* me at the Life Directions seminar."

"Oh, wow. That's pretty funny."

"Indeed."

Maribel and I continued talking, and after the meeting ended, we agreed to work together. Every idea that we had discussed had prompted a resounding *YES* in my mind. We set up a second meeting to design a program and an online marketing plan.

In about six weeks—record time—we had designed a full-service program with a script and all the necessary written elements, had designed a workbook for students, had created a joint venture invite list, and had written all sales copy and email invites. We had scheduled our joint venture marketing campaign calendar all the way through our first free call program launch teleseminar, and we had created and signed a memorandum of understanding agreement.

Meeting Maribel felt like it was clearly part of a divine design. We were in sync from our first meeting. We spent a good amount of time talking about what each of us wanted the program to be, as well as what we didn't want it to be. We ended up with a great list that perfectly represented the character of this new endeavor.

I am honored to say we have stayed true to this list for the duration of our business relationship. We designed and implemented a program that teaches everything you would ever need to know about writing a book, from first thought to bestseller.

What we created is now the *Bake Your Book Program,* named in honor of the conversation Maura and I had when we started planning *Who Do You Think You Are?*

Remember?

Maura had said, "That book idea is half-baked," and I responded, "Well, we better bake it quickly."

It is what I still consider the best group mentor program for book writing ever created. We ran this program for years, and over that time, we helped hundreds, possibly thousands, to write and market their books. We built a community of authors. Today, we offer this program as a home-study course.

After the book-mentoring program got off the ground, it seemed like all our business projects were finally going well. Our lives appeared to be getting back to normal. I was at my best yet, professionally, and finally felt like I was living into my purpose on a daily basis.

I didn't know what was coming next, but I could feel that every step—each project and each new encounter—was moving me forward, in the direction designed by my angels.

Mom Again

Maura and I settled into a routine. For the first time, we had some stability and regularity in our lives. No sooner did we realize this than we received a call from a doctor at the facility where my mother lived.

The doctor informed us that my mother was refusing to eat. For weeks, she had been on liquid foods because she wouldn't put her teeth in, but now she refused to eat at all. This tends to happen when people are ready to die, and that's what the staff assumed was happening. Her body was already shutting down, and she wasn't talking anymore. She was only responding with head movements and seemed disoriented. We were told we needed to discuss hospice options, and make sure my mom's advance medical directive was in order and up-to-date.

So much was going through my head as I was told this news. First, I couldn't believe what I was hearing. I was feeling grateful they had called me. I was feeling scared for my mother. I knew her better than anyone did, however, and I felt sure I could help her. I had been witness to so many of her ups and downs in my childhood; I knew, first hand, what Mom was capable of surviving.

I got myself together and went into her room.

I was completely honest with her. I told her what the doctor had told me and that, if she kept going the way she was, she had only a few weeks left to live. At this news, my mom's eyes opened as up as wide as silver dollars. I asked her if she wanted to die, and she shook her head furiously from side to side. I told her I was now in charge of her care, and she needed to trust me.

Maura and I stepped out of Mom's room and headed out to the car. I called Dr. Bob, a client and dear friend of mine. I trusted him, more than anyone else, to help me create a plan.

He told me that first, I needed to get her off the medicines that weren't helping her and get as many vitamins into her as possible. He recommended a hospice care nurse and that Mom start drinking Ensure, a chocolate milk drink with extra nutrients. Then, we were to get her off all medications except the ones for pain. In fact, she needed to go on morphine to mask the side effects of coming off years of drugs. This was to go on for thirty days and then, we were to wean her off the morphine. Drinking Ensure would sustain her nutritionally during this time.

We followed Dr. Bob's plan to the letter, and a few weeks later, she was off the morphine and speaking clearly. She put her brand new set of false teeth back in her mouth, and asked the nurses to transition her from blended food to solids over the course of a few days. Mom came back remarkably strong. Honestly, I had not seen her this clear in her head, speech, or actions in ten years. It was amazing to see her recovery unfold. Not only had my mother survived, which nobody had predicted, she had come back stronger, sharper, and more motivated than ever.

It wasn't long before she was back on solid food and asking to get out of bed. She wanted to see which of her friends were still there, and to see who had passed away while she was out of it. She felt it was important to get out of bed as much as possible.

A week or so later, the physical therapist asked Mom if she'd like to start working on walking. She had been in a wheel chair for a long time, but she agreed to try, and learning to walk again was her focus for some time. Her goal was to walk with a walker.

Once she was doing well, I thought she might want to move out of the full-care facility and into assisted living, but she surprised us by saying she liked the place, and wanted to stay.

She asked me to go through her things in the storage facility, sell some, and bring some of them to her at the facility so she could give them away to her friends.

Welcome back, my crazy Mom.

To Move or Not to Move

On a beautiful summer day in Santa Barbara, Maura and I attended a dear friend's installation ceremony—she was being ordained as a minister. While in her office, I noticed framed pictures of trees. The leaves on the trees were red, orange, yellow, purple, and green. I asked Maura how she thought the artist had achieved that effect.

I had genuinely been thinking that the photographer used photo-editing software to get those colors.

Yes, I was over forty, and I had never seen autumn leaves in full color. Remember, I'm from California, where the leaves are green all year round.

Maura laughed and told me about fall foliage. She made a plan to take me back to Vermont, so I could see it myself. She called her mother, and they hatched a plan. Maura figured that, while we were in Vermont, she could show me around some of the towns surrounding her parents' home. While searching for places to visit, she also came across a beautiful house for sale.

We flew to Boston, and once we landed, we took the same bus—to White River Junction—that we had taken when I met her parents the first time. As we boarded the bus and headed out, I saw trees with a little bit of color. The further north we went, the more colors appeared in the trees. I had never seen such beauty.

At the bus station in Vermont, Maura's mom explained that leaf season was just starting in that part of Vermont. She assured me, as Maura had, that I had not seen anything yet. We settled in at Maura's parents' house, and went for a walk to soak up some of the beautiful color. We relaxed for the rest of the day, just spending time with Mom and Dad and catching up.

The next day, Maura and I went on an adventure to a lake that is visible in the distance from her parents' deck. We parked and hiked the trail and up a mountain. Neither of us was in great shape, but we hiked like two teenagers on a mission. I took pictures the whole way. I felt as though I must be the most blessed man on the face of the earth.

We continued hiking, and Maura started to get excited.

Finally, she said, "We're here."

There was a group of people ahead of us. Once they left, Maura led me out to a rocky ledge. Thank goodness, I was no longer afraid of heights. The view was spectacular.

Throughout the rest of the vacation, which included a trip to Canada where the foliage was further along, Rita, Maura's mother, kept dropping strong hints about how wonderful it would be if we moved to Vermont. The rents were reasonable. There were lots of artists and writers. And it was so very beautiful.

Maura and I visited Montpelier, the state capital, as well as Burlington. Montpelier is the least populous capital in the country. The main part of town is only one square mile. As soon as we arrived in Montpelier, my mind started doing the strangest thing. It was like something from the movie, *The Terminator*. My mind was tuning into only certain aspects of the town. I would notice something, and then the screen in my mind would draw a square around it and zoom in, bringing focus only to that one thing.

First, I noticed there were three bookstores, all within a few blocks of each other. I also noticed that, because the city was so small, everything—from the political offices to the media—was accessible. It was all so different from the experience of living within the enormity of California, and it was blowing my mind.

As I walked through the town, my brain gradually drifted into business contemplations. For some time in California, I had been reaching out to teen organizations and teen non-profits, in an effort to advocate for the youth population. I offered my speaking services at no charge and offered to give all the teens a free copy of *Who Do You Think You Are?* Rarely did I even get a reply.

We had a warehouse full of those books I wanted teens to have. I had been feeling frustrated, as if I were one of a million fish in a sea of saturation.

I mused: *Here, in this small town, I would be a big fish in a small pond.*

No sooner did I have that thought than I heard a voice say: *This is where you are supposed to be.*

I looked over my shoulder to see who was there. It had been a while since my last contact with an angel, and I was out of practice.

I said, "What?"

Again, I heard: *This is where you're supposed to be. This is where you take your next steps.*

I looked at Maura and said, "I just heard the voice, and it said this is where I'm supposed to be."

She wasn't surprised. She had just found herself looking at a house outside of town with no logical reason why she was doing it.

"That explains a lot," she said.

We continued to walk the town while my business mind dreamed up ways I could be of service to a small community. There was a high school and two colleges. This trip was blowing my mind, and we hadn't even looked at the house yet.

Maura said, "I had a feeling that this was going to be the town you would be drawn to."

After our walk, we looked at the house Maura had found. It was beautiful on the outside. There was no For Sale sign on the lawn and we didn't have an appointment, so we just admired it from the road.

We headed to Burlington, which was more like the beach towns where I had grown up. It was beautiful and romantic because I was walking with my lovely wife, Maura, but didn't have the juice for me that Montpelier did.

After the day we'd had, I was now very interested in moving to Vermont. Once the conversation started to get serious, Maura reminded me that winters were cold and long. If she would ever consider moving here, it would be with the one condition that I would get her the heck out of Vermont for the winters. We started to brainstorm how it would work if we moved. We made a list of positive and negative reasons for the move.

There were many wonderful reasons to move but there were three big reasons to stay in California:

1. Mom
2. My son, and my nephew, whom I had raised
3. Agape

Maura had been there for me, and for my family, for quite a while, and we had only traveled a few times to be with her family. Her father was suffering with some health problems, and I felt like it was her time to be with her family.

Additionally, I had been taking care of my family my whole life. I always rushed to assist the family, and I was beginning to feel like it was time for me to do something I wanted to do.

At twelve years old, I'd had a vision, and in that vision, I was living in the mountains, in a house surrounded by trees, with a smoking hot wife, enjoying my life.

Wasn't it *my* time yet?

I had been clearly instructed, "This is where you're supposed to be."

Maura and I shared all our feelings with each other. We debated both sides and continued to add to our lists all the way back to California. No matter what spin we put on it, there were far more reasons to move than to stay. By the time we got home, we had made our decision. We were moving to Vermont.

No sooner had we set the date than there was a knock on our door.

"Who is it?"

"The Long Beach Police Department."

15

A Parent's Worst Nightmare and Expecting a Miracle

My son, Timar, was at Memorial Hospital. He'd been assaulted, had a head wound, and was unconscious.

We rushed to the car and sped over to Memorial Hospital in record time. At the ER, we were directed to an empty room where a doctor joined us.

"Here is what we know so far. Your son was picked up on the Pacific Coast Highway with a head wound. He was taken to Community Hospital, was awake, and was able to answer questions. Then, his eyes suddenly rolled up in the back of his head, which is a red flag—it can indicate brain bleeding—but Community Hospital had neither the equipment needed, nor a surgeon on shift to treat a brain bleed, so they immediately transferred him to us."

He went on to tell us that, while Timar was on his way to Memorial Hospital, one of their doctors, who happened to be the best brain surgeon on the west coast, had been about to leave for the day, but stayed when he was told there was an emergency case coming his way.

The doctor continued, "Timar was here in this room for all of two minutes before being rushed to emergency surgery. He's in the operating room right now. He has the best surgeon possible, and all we can do now is wait and hope. If you'll follow me, I'm going to take you to the OR waiting room. There is an officer waiting for you there who'd like to ask you some questions. We're still trying to figure out exactly what happened to your boy—so far it's a bit of a mystery."

"Okay."

I didn't know what else to say. Maura and I were in shock, both somewhat speechless as we stood up and followed the doctor to the officer who was waiting for us.

He introduced himself and explained that Timar was riding his bicycle with blood running down the side of his head when an officer spotted him. Timar couldn't or wouldn't explain what had happened to him. The officer had him taken to Community Hospital. The police did not know who had assaulted my son but they were doing their best to find out.

Maura flipped through the contacts in her phone to find someone we could call for support and asked me, "Should I call Shaman Mary?"

"Yes. Please call her. That's a great idea."

Shaman Mary Raymakers is a good friend of ours. She is a world-renowned Master Sacred Shaman who does everything from soul retrieval to releasing phobias to healing past pain and trauma, both physical and emotional. When she heard what had happened, she left the restaurant where she was having dinner with her husband to talk to us. She took the phone to her car, and spoke to Maura, who reported to me what she said.

First, Mary took a series of deep breaths and tuned in. She told us Timar was out of his body, and she would find him. After a while, she located him and reminded him who she was. She told Timar he needed to follow her because he needed to get back to his body. She told him he'd had an accident, but it wasn't his time to leave. He was to use this experience to lift him, and to propel him to another level of consciousness.

She took him back to his body. Once in the operating room, Mary reported she'd never seen so many angels in one place. It was incredibly bright, and there were angels guiding the doctors' hands.

After a time, she said, "Timar's back in his body."

Maura continued to tell me what Mary was saying, "The doctor is finishing and just said, 'Great job everyone. He's alive; we've done all we can do. Now, it's up to him.' He's going to scrub out and then, will meet with the family."

Maura stopped talking and said, "Mary wants to know if you have any questions for her."

I did. Maura handed me the phone.

"Mary—first of all—thank you so much for getting Timar back to the operating room. Thank you for returning him to his body."

"You're welcome."

"While we wait for the doctor, my question is, what can I do for Timar? What can I do to support him?"

She told me to breathe and close my eyes, and then she guided me with the following instructions:

> *I want you to see your boy with his eyes open. He's looking at you, he sees you, and he loves you. Now create a tube or a cord that goes from your navel to his. It is connecting the two of you. Look him in his eyes, and tell him the following, 'This is my life*

> *force, my love, my power. Use me. You can use as much as you want—I have plenty for both of us. I am here for you. Even in the fog, you can find me; even through the fog, I will find you. I love you. You are going to make it through this. Use me, son. I am here for you. You're going to make it through this.*

She told me, "Keith, it's going to be really ugly for a while. Things are not going to look good on the outside, and people will try to tell you things that aren't true. Know this: by the third day, there will be a shift, and once the shift happens, healing will begin to proceed at a rapid pace. Nurses and doctors will be amazed, and he will be up and out of there before you know it. This wasn't supposed to happen. It was not his fate to die at a young age. He's going to make it, and you must stay strong and have faith. Do you have any other questions for me at this time?"

"No. Just, thank you. I appreciate you right now."

"No problem, Keith. Keep me in the loop, and let me know if I can help you further."

"Thank you. Thank you, Mary."

It seemed to take forever, but the surgeon arrived and explained that Timar had been struck with an object, and that he had an epidural hematoma, also known as an epidural hemorrhage. They'd done everything they could for him in the OR, but Timar was not out of the woods yet. He was still alive and breathing, but they did not know if he would ever wake up. If he did, they didn't know if he would be able to speak, or if he would have his motor functions. Only time would reveal the answers to these questions.

Maura looked at the doctor and said, "We know that Timar is going to be just fine. We are expecting a full recovery. We are expecting nothing less than 100 percent full recovery, and we will accept nothing less."

I asked him if he was on board with that, and the doctor replied, "I can make no promises, but I can surely join you in hoping and wishing for the best for him. I will do that for him."

"That's all we can ask for. Thank you."

"Now, you can head to the intensive care unit, and when he's ready for you, you'll be able to be with your boy there."

Maura and I embraced as the doctor walked away. We got up and headed up to ICU where a small sign told us to pick up the phone, and wait for a nurse to answer. I picked up the phone, and there was no answer. I waited—still no answer. Someone came out the door, so I ran over, caught the door, and we snuck in.

Somehow, I was well ahead of Maura, so I entered the room first, and saw my son on the bed with a nurse next to him. Timar was uncovered and lay naked, lifeless, with tubes and machines breathing for him. The sight was horrible.

The nurse turned and said, "I need you to wait outside until I come get you."

Maura did her best to calm me as we headed back to the waiting room.

Eventually, the nurse came out to get us and said to me, gently, "Now you know why we have people wait until we're ready."

She brought us to the room where Timar was and told us he was in a medically-induced coma. She shared that the brain was swollen from the surgery, and the pain from the surgery would be too much for anyone to endure.

She said, "At this point, even if he wanted to, he couldn't come out of it. We are using the drugs to allow him to rest and to recover."

She told us they would be watching for signs that would tell them he was ready to come out of it. She went on to say that these types of recoveries were like a marathon and not a sprint—it would take time. She suggested that we go home and get some sleep.

"It may be the last good night's sleep you will get for a very long time. There is no way to know what's going to happen, or how long it will take."

Maura and I were hesitant to leave his side, although seeing his seemingly lifeless body lying on the bed there was slowly ripping my heart wide open.

The nurse promised us he would make it through the night.

"If anything out of the ordinary happens, I will call you immediately. If you give yourself this gift of one good night's sleep, it may help you for the next few days when you may be up all night. Please, trust me."

After checking in with each other and feeling into what felt right, we decided to trust her, to drive home and try to get some sleep. I was on autopilot. I was driving but I was thinking of nothing but Timar. I kept flashing on the scene I walked into in the ICU.

Maura interrupted my thoughts saying, "Keith, look around us. Look at what we're driving through."

Surrounding the car was a thick fog, and visibility was extremely limited.

"Remember what Mary had you say to Timar? *I am here for you. Even in the fog, you can find me; even through the fog, I will find you.* And now we are driving through the fog to get home.

When we arrived home, we tried to contact Timar's mother, but it turned out that we had an old phone number for her. We did our best to sleep, but not a lot of rest was had on that dark night.

The next morning, we headed immediately to the hospital and to Timar's room. It still looked like there was nothing happening. I didn't see signs of any life other than the machine breathing for him. It was terribly hard to witness, and I started to break down.

Maura put her arms around me.

"Honey, we have it from a reliable source that Timar is going to be fine—remember? This is the part when things look bad, but we need to be strong for him right now. We are accepting only 100 percent full recovery."

She held me close and said, "If at any point you waver, I need you to leave the room. Do what you need to do—cry, breathe, pray—and when you are back to believing in perfect health for Timar, come back. Matter of fact, why don't you go take a break right now?"

I excused myself, went to the waiting room, and fell apart, sobbing and crying while others in the waiting room witnessed my pain. Eventually, I collected myself and redirected my thoughts—away from fear and toward the Truth. I picked up the phone, gained entry back into the ICU, and entered Timar's room.

Maura smiled at me, "You all right? You back with me?"

"Yes, honey, thanks for that. I just needed to let some of it out."

"I completely understand. We can't have that for him, though. We'll need to monitor it. Let everyone who comes into this room know about it."

"Got it."

I was—and still am—completely blown away by Maura's clarity and strength during this time. She kept it together enough for the three of us. For everyone.

Throughout the day, nurses fussed with the tubes, changed IV bags, and monitored Timar constantly. They kept smiling at us with compassion and an obvious understanding of what we were experiencing. A few hours later, my mind started to wander again, and I started to spin down the tunnel of despair. I felt the blood start to drain from my face. Just then, an orderly came into the room. He was a young and handsome black man.

He looked at me directly and said, "He's going to be all right. He's young, he's strong, and he's a fighter. He's going be all right. You can count on that. He's going to be all right."

He walked out of the room. Something in his voice told me that this man truly believed what he had said. It was exactly what I needed to hear in that moment. I lifted my head and stepped back into knowing and seeing Timar's perfect healing.

The nurse entered the room and said, "You have some visitors."

I walked out to the waiting room and found our dear friends, Kelly and John, who were members of the church where Timar was a youth teacher on Sunday mornings. John was a mind-body expert, a shamanic drummer, and an energy healer.

John asked me, "Can I work on him?" and of course, I agreed.

He came in, stood next to Timar with his eyes closed for some time, and then he started slowly moving his hands over Timar's body. He started down at his feet. He took his hands and moved them in a circular motion over Timar, and it looked like he was energetically pulling energy out of Timar. He would then close his hand, pull it to the side and make a motion like he was tossing the negative energy aside, then he'd return to the body and start the process again. He did this from Timar's feet all the way up.

When he moved his hands up over Timar's head, he did the swirling motion and when he made that movement to pull the energy out, Timar sat straight up, his head precisely following the motion of John's hand.

He opened his eyes, turned his head, looked at John, and smiled as if to say: *Oh, it's you. Okay.*

He promptly lay back, closed his eyes, and returned to the way he was.

I said, "Holy crap, that was intense."

John says, "I know—right?"

It was amazing.

John completed his process, put his hand on Timar's heart for a minute, bowed to Timar, and walked out to the waiting room. The four of us visited for a while before they left.

I reached out to family, friends, and mentors via the phone, caught them up on what was happening, and asked them all for prayer support for Timar. I asked them to pray specifically for 100 percent recovery. It was hard to repeat the story of what had happened, but I knew it was important to get the word out.

One dear mentor and friend promised she would reach out to the most renowned healers in the world, and assured me they would all be working on Timar remotely. I posted on Facebook, asking for prayer, and it was spreading worldwide.

Prayer Warriors from all over the world were posting and re-posting, "Timar needs your support and prayers." We felt the love, all around us.

After an extremely long day, we were tired and drained. Walking into Timar's room after saying goodbye to another friend, my eyes started to well up. Once again, I could feel my faith slipping. I looked up and there was the orderly, standing by Timar, looking at me, and shaking his head.

He said, "Man, I'm telling you, he's going to be all right. He's young, he's strong, and he's a fighter, this one. Look at him; he's going be all right. You can count on that," and he walked out of the room.

After four days, the nurse told us it was time to bring him out of the coma.

She said, "Then, we'll see how it goes."

A little time passed, and Timar showed signs of movement. He started to moan and squirm a bit as though he was experiencing pain and discomfort. I was so happy he showed signs of life I didn't think to be upset about the pain.

That night at the ICU was the longest night of our lives. None of us slept. Timar was moaning, writhing, flipping, pulling the covers off, and we had to do whatever we could to keep him from tearing out his brain drain, his IV, and his catheter.

Maura and I took turns trying to doze off while the other played the game we called, "Keep the boy from ripping stuff out." After a while, it became apparent that our strategy wasn't working.

As I had learned to do from my angels, I changed my way of thinking—by asking a different question. Everything you manifest into your existence is a direct result of the quality of the questions you ask.

Instead of worrying about what would happen if he pulled the tubes out, I started to focus on this question: *What can we do to make sure they stay in?*

It worked. Timar seemed to relax a little more as we focused our attention on the image of the tubes staying in. Just changing the question had helped, just as the angels had taught me.

Even so, it was painful for us both to see him so miserable. The night went on forever. I was scheduled to sing at a church service the next morning. Although it was about an hour south of the hospital, I felt, with every part of my inner knowing, that my son would want me to keep this gig. I had been up all night, but I think, deep down, there was a part of me that needed to let some of this pain out, and, in addition, I badly needed prayer support.

In the morning, I kissed Maura and Timar goodbye and went to the house to pick up my guitar and equipment. I packed up the car and headed to the church.

When I arrived at the church, my dear friend, Reverend Les Demarco, greeted me warmly. He embraced me and told me that, not only had he been praying; he had also sent out an email to every practitioner he knew. Shortly after that, the guest speaker arrived. Her name was Kathy Hearn, the Community Spiritual Leader of United Centers for Spiritual Living. She said Les had called her the night before to tell her about Timar. She had sent out an email to every Reverend in the whole movement asking that each one of them include Timar in their prayers during their church service.

So many people were praying for Timar's recovery.

Somehow, I made it through the service. I sang the song, *I Don't Need to Know,* by Daniel Nahmod, and dedicated it to Timar. After service, I collected what seemed like a hundred hugs, packed up my guitar, put it in the car, and went to the room where people meet after service to eat and connect. I needed to get some food into my body before I left. Les and my dear friend and spiritual practitioner, Joe Seoane, were planning to go with me to the hospital after I ate. I continued to connect with people as I nibbled at some food.

After a few minutes, Les came into the doorway of the room and announced, "I just got a call from Maura. She said Timar is awake and doing well."

We were a one-phone family at that point, and Maura had our phone to keep in communication with friends and family.

Les continued, "When they pulled the tube out of his mouth, his first words were, 'Can I get a coffee?' followed by, 'Where's my dad?' "

I immediately replied, "Well, at least he's got his priorities straight!"

The room lit up in laughter, and as applause broke out in the room, a wave of relief washed over me.

I finished eating and Les said, "You should head out. Joe and I will be right behind you after I wrap things up here."

When I arrived at hospital, Maura shared with me what I had missed.

She said, "After they removed the tube from Timar's throat, he gestured to me to come closer. I put my ear up to his mouth, and he whispered, 'Can I get a coffee?' Inside, I was laughing and crying at the same time. I was never so glad to hear any words in my life. I felt a wave of relief, joy, shock, and gratefulness, all at the same time."

Maura still had tears in her eyes as she continued, "Then he gestured again. I leaned in, and he asked 'Where's Dad?' I told him you were singing at the church, and you'd be coming in a while. The next time I left Timar's side, I went back out to the lobby and called Les. Then I called my mom and bawled my face off because I was so happy and relieved."

She smiled and said, "By the way, he's been trying to get that cup of coffee ever since."

From the moment I arrived, Timar was trying to get the nurses to track down the doctor.

When the doctor arrived, he introduced himself, "I'm Dr. Thomas, shift doctor today. What can I do for you?"

Timar shook the doctor's hand. "Hey, Doc. Pleasure to meet you. My name is Timar Smith. Nice place you've got here. I'm just wondering, how long you think it's going to be before I can get out of here?"

The doctor laughed out loud, "Well, you did just wake up from a coma. We're going to have to observe you, and you will have to pass a number of tests before you can leave. The answer to your question is—I'm not sure. Perhaps you should slow down a little bit, son. For now, we'll get a good meal in you and take it from there."

"How about a cup of coffee, Doc? I've been trying to get one since I woke up."

The doctor grinned and turned to the nurse, "Nurse, how about we get this young man a cup of coffee?"

He finally did get his cup of coffee—and promptly spilled some on himself. We were surprised they would give coffee to someone who had just woken up from a coma, but Timar was adamant about what he wanted. I think getting what he asked for helped.

Timar was in rare form.

He told me, "Damn, I need to pee."

I said, "Go right ahead. You have a catheter in you."

"No, I don't. Do I?"

He looked under the covers and saw the catheter.

"God damn it."

Maura and I tried our best not to laugh.

The nurses came in about a half an hour later to take the catheter out. She was stunningly beautiful. Timar immediately started flirting with her.

"Wow, you're gorgeous. Do you have a boyfriend?"

"Yes, I do," she answered.

"Too bad. That's a damn shame."

She excused us from the room so they could take out the catheter. We gladly stepped out.

I thought to myself: *I've been traumatized enough without seeing that.*

After catheter removal, they encouraged Timar to go for a stroll around the ICU floor, with me by his side. We started walking. Timar flirted with every woman we saw and asked out three of them. By that evening, they moved Timar out of ICU and into his own room.

The next morning, Maura headed to the hospital by herself. I had a teleseminar scheduled with Maribel for our book-writing program. Maura said she'd wait until after the call and let me know how things were going at the hospital.

The teleseminar lasted about ninety minutes. I had two messages waiting for me from Maura when we were done. The first was to tell me how well Timar was doing on all the medical tests. The second was to tell me they'd discharged him.

We could bring Timar home.

I was in shock, and very excited. It was hard to believe it had been just four days from emergency brain surgery to full recovery and release. All our prayers had been answered.

When I arrived at the hospital, they were still talking to Timar, having him sign paperwork. While he finished the discharge process, Maura and I decided we'd go upstairs to the ICU to thank everyone for taking care of Timar.

The nurse who was working the day we first arrived was there. We told her Timar was being kicked out already, and that he had passed every test they had thrown at him—with flying colors.

She looked at us with her eyes welling up and said, "That's why I do this job. Every once in a while I get to witness a miracle!"

As I thanked a few other nurses, I asked if I could speak to the orderly who had been there for me the two times I needed it the most. She asked me to describe the man.

I did and she said, "Nobody on this floor fits that description."

Maura and I looked at each other and realized that yet another angel had taken physical form to be there when I was in dire need of support. I was glad that, this time, Maura had shared the experience with me.

Timar's recovery was a bit of a roller coaster ride. His head was filled with staples, so there were moments when he couldn't even finish a thought, as well as moments of brilliance. As recommended by his doctors, I purchased car models, puzzles, and anything that stimulated the brain without making him think too much. We had a near constant flow of friends coming to see him. After the first day, we began moderating his visitors so he wouldn't get overwhelmed.

On Timar's second day at home, we asked Dr. George Gonzalez, the creator of Quantum Neurology, to come check Timar's neurological functions.

When he finished, he said, "Young man. I want make sure you are clear about what you've been given. You've truly been given a second chance. A miracle has occurred, and I believe it has happened so that you can do something profound with your life. You still have staples in your head, you're five days out from a blunt head trauma, and neurologically, you are in better shape than anyone who walks into my office. Do you understand how important it is that you do something with this?"

Timar assured him the miracle had not been wasted on him, and he promised the doctor he would make the most out of it.

Timar eventually confided in us about what happened the night he was injured. He had been in the wrong place, at the wrong time, with the wrong people. I won't go into detail, because it's not my story to tell. It's not what's relevant here anyway.

Crises happen to all of us. Think about the ones that have happened to you in the past. Instead of focusing on the actual event, think about these questions:

What did you do in response?

What changes came out of the crisis?

Life is long—hopefully—and it's not the things that happen to you that will define you. No, your true self can be seen in how you *react* to what happens to you.

It's how Timar was able to recover and move forward with his life that will always be the most important part of this story.

Timar's recovery period is a blur of memories for me. Each and every moment was cherished and appreciated. It was a joy to see him embracing the miracle and planning how he would speak to other young people about what he had experienced. He wanted to use what had happened to him to take him to his next level of transformation. He wanted to make a difference in the lives of others.

Vermont Here We Come

Once Timar was clearly on the mend, Maura and I returned to planning for our move to Vermont. Timar decided he'd move to Oregon to be with his mom.

For me, the hardest part of our move from California to Vermont was telling my nephew and my mother. My nephew took it hard at first but ultimately he understood, even though my leaving meant adding his name to his grandmother's health directive and having almost no family nearby.

My mother did not take it well. She was angry and acted out, like a child, as if I had done something bad to her in just mentioning a move. It wasn't until I shared how important it was that we be there for Maura's aging father that she reluctantly agreed. We packed our belongings and said our goodbyes.

Our preparations for this trip east had been filled with so many moments of challenge that, if it weren't for clarity of vision and purpose, I might have wondered if we made the right decision.

But we were sure, very sure, and as we crossed into Vermont, we were holding hands.

When we arrived at Maura's parents' home, we spent ten days with them before they headed to Spain for February through April. We stayed and took care of their house while they were away, which gave us some stress-free time to look for our perfect place in Vermont.

Maura thoroughly researched the towns near Montpelier to find our new home.

It was where the voice had told me, "This is where you are supposed to be."

From over thirty options, we chose two to see one Friday.

In the morning, we woke up with excited anticipation. Many times in the past, Maura and I had set out on journeys like this one, and we had prepared for it the way we had learned to do. We listed all the qualities and physical aspects of what we are looking for and then focused on what we called the *best possible outcome* (BPO). We prayed on it, and then let it go, knowing it would come to pass just as we had created it—or even better.

The first house was beautiful—a five-bedroom and five-bath mountain home that sat on fifty acres of woods—but it didn't feel like a match. As we discussed it, we realized it felt empty, and we didn't like the push for a decision from the owner. In addition, we learned that there would be little to no internet connection at that location.

I looked inward, and then said to Maura, "The next place is the one we're supposed to see."

Tree House

We got in the car and headed to the next house in the town of Waitsfield. As we drove past the town sign, it was as if we had hit a time warp. I felt as though I'd driven through a wall of energy and everything had slowed down for just a moment. Then we were kicked out of that energy as if tossed forward. We started to notice and point out things as we drove around the town.

First thing we saw was a cable company on the right hand side of the road. That was one concern taken care of immediately. As we drove around, we looked at all the small stores, businesses, and restaurants. The stores were almost all independent establishments, as opposed to chain stores. The town had just about everything we could or would need.

We pulled up to the house. It was the perfect distance from town.

The house was all wood, no particular color, just old wood gray. It was a tall house. As we stepped up on the porch, it loomed above us—up and up and up, like a tree house.

We entered the code the owners had given us into the key lockbox, I turned the key, and we stepped through the front door. Another wave of energy swept over me.

"This is it," I said. "This is the place."

I had been in that place so many times in my mind that I already knew it well. Being inside the house felt exactly the way I had dreamed it when I was twelve. It was the place I had visited, time after time, in my meditation and visioning sessions.

Maura fell in love with the place at once. We wandered about the house, happily, from room to room, and then walked around the lovely quiet property.

There was no doubt in either of our minds; this was our place.

She asked me, "What do you want to do? Shall we leave a note saying we love the place and want to talk about leasing it?

The owners wouldn't be back for another five hours, but I couldn't just leave a note. This was too important—and I was too excited.

I replied, "There's no way I'm leaving here until this place is ours! Let's go explore, have dinner, and wait for them."

Maura agreed. We went back to our little town and drove some smaller roads to see what was around. The more we saw, the more it all felt like a perfect match for us. I could still sense that wave of energy all around, and could feel our complete alignment with it. After eating, we went back to the house to wait.

The owners, a husband and wife, arrived late, but we waited for them. We didn't even talk about leaving. When they did arrive, they were surprised to see us in the driveway. It didn't take long for them to sense our excitement about the place. We discussed the place and the lease contract possibilities.

After we had answered all the questions they had about us, and about our business, the wife said, "As far as we are concerned, if you want the place, it's yours."

Even before she finished her sentence, we were replying with a resounding, "Yes."

We ended up sketching out the lease in pencil on a piece of paper.

The husband owner said, "Welcome to Vermont. That's the way things are done around here."

It was a wonderful end to an amazing day.

It was a milestone in an amazing journey.

So many years had passed—so many heartaches, fears, joys, and crises. So many decisions had been made to bring us along our paths, separate and together, ending at this place.

Turn the pages back in this book now, and you can reread the plan I had made for my life when I was twelve.

I told my friend's dad—do you remember?

I was going to live in the mountains, in a five-bedroom, four-bathroom home, with a beautiful wife.

I was going to be a musician in my twenties and thirties and a bestselling author and speaker in my forties.

As Maura and I stood in our Tree House that day, I realized, in that moment, that *it had all come to pass*. I had everything I had envisioned so long ago. I had created my perfect world and my perfect place.

Life was good and all was well. I had lived to see my dreams come true.

None of this would have happened without my angels.

Angels had told me my purpose, giving me direction and a reason to go on when life was hard. Angels had shown me how to ask the right questions to help me make good decisions. Angels, many times, pointed me toward the right steps to take along the way. And, of course, angels kept me alive in the first place, saving my life many times, or I would never would have made it this far.

I have learned to take the time to listen to my guardian angels, in all forms. I have learned to act on their advice, to take the next steps as they are received.

Because of my angels, I have lived my life in great fullness, in service to others. I have found mentors for every area of my life, and I have been a mentor to many. I have managed the ups and downs of the business world and have experienced success as a business owner. With the help of my angels, I have responded to adversity with grace and resilience, have cared for my family deeply, and have loved unconditionally.

I have seen some amazing things—miracles, you might call them—but do you know what strikes me as most astounding?

It is the joy.

It is the pure joy of living this blessed life.

Conclusion

And Now . . .

We have lived in the mountains of Vermont for four years, and I truly love the country life.

Except for the Vermont winters.

We stayed a full winter just once, because I wanted to see what everyone was complaining about. Unfortunately, the winter that I talked Maura into staying for ended up being the coldest winter on record in a hundred years.

Needless to say, that was the last winter we spent here. We now live in Vermont six months of the year, and we spend winters in other places. We've found these winter places using the same process we used to manifest our Tree House.

My life continues to be blessed by angels. I am prompted often and pointed toward next steps to take, just as I have described in this book.

As you know now, this book was angel-inspired and spirit-led. There are angels among us. They are here to guide us, but cannot be noticed or heard until you open your mind and heart to them. Whether or not you invite them into your life, they will have an effect on your life, but if you invite them in, what a difference they can make!

I have a unique perspective because I have lived my life both with angels and without them. I can tell you, without hesitation, that I prefer my life with the angels.

After reading this book, do you now believe in angels?

Do you believe in the possibility that they exist?

Did this book help you realize that some parts of your life have already been touched by angels?

Or, do you think I should seek professional help?

Either way, now that you are at the end of the book, it is my hope that you feel better than when you picked it up!

I am out of the angel closet now. For years, I told almost no one about my experiences with angels. When I did, I noticed that whomever I shared my stories with needed to hear them right at that moment. Each story was perfectly timed for the person listening. This encouraged me to use my inner guidance. Whenever I am prompted, I share the story I was prompted to share, and it always seems to make a difference in the listener's life.

For years, I'd had a fear of sharing my stories. I thought people would think I was crazy and might lock me up. Believe it or not, they used to lock people up who heard voices in their head. By the time I started sharing my stories, however, the world had changed. Many stories that would have previously been dismissed as supernatural nonsense were being written about, reported, and discussed in groups.

By the time I was brave enough to recount what had happened to me, most of the people I shared my experiences with were accepting, and it was a welcome surprise.

Angels don't appear to me physically anymore, which makes sense. They had only done so to help me believe. I needed to see physical proof in the beginning—over, and over again. Now, because I know they exist, all they need to do is whisper in my ear. I hear the voice, and I do as I am instructed. This practice has been life changing for me, for my business, and for my relationships.

We all have at least one guardian angel assigned to us. I have many. I am moved to share with you one last story.

Many years back, I was at an event filled with inspirational speakers. In between listening to presentations, I was out milling with the crowd, and I noticed that a group of people had gathered around a woman. As I passed by, I heard her talking about her experience with angels. People were hanging on her every word. I came to find out that she was a well-known angel expert.

I stood about fifty feet away and watched her interact with the group around her.

She turned to look my way, her eyes got big, and she looked at me and mouthed the words, "We need to talk."

Time passed, and she excused herself from the group surrounding her. She came to me, looked me in the eye, and said, "Do you, by any chance, believe in angels?"

"You mean them?" I pointed over my shoulder.

"Thank God. I've never seen so many assigned to one person in my life."

"Yeah, I call them my posse. Believe me when I tell you, I know they are there!"

She asked me more questions—and it felt so good to be able to share stories with someone who not only believed in my angels, but also was able to physically see them.

I am a blessed man, a happy man, and a loving man, who is now fully living into his purpose. I should have been dead at least seven times before, but I'm still here. To all of you who have touched my life over the years, I give my heartfelt thanks. For those of you who have taken the time to read our books, have written books with us, have worked with me personally, or who have allowed me to be your angel, I am grateful.

I am here for a purpose. You are part of that purpose, and that is a gift for both of us.

Thanks for being the unique gift that is *you*. You make a difference in this world, whether you have realized it or not.

I trust that you are clear on this now: *This world would not be the same without you.*

You are here at this particular time for a reason. You are a light for others. One smile, one hug, or one *hello* can make a difference to someone. Open up to the possibilities, and notice the angels all around you. You make a difference!

It is my hope that you are now feeling encouraged, inspired, and motivated to walk and talk with your angels. If you don't already have a connection with angels, now is the perfect time to make the connection.

In this moment, stop reading, close your eyes, and slowly take three deep breaths.

When you are ready, open your mind and your heart right now, and say—

> *Dear Angels,*
>
> *I am open to your guidance and your wisdom. I am grateful for all you've done and I want you to know that I'm now listening. I am looking for you. I am listening for you.*
>
> *Guide me, instruct me, and show me all the ways I can be, do, and have all that I am to be, do, or have in this life. How may I be of service? How may I live into my purpose? Show me the way.*
>
> *I am grateful for your support. And so it is.*
>
> *Thank you, thank you, thank you.*

And thank *you*, dear reader, for taking this beautiful journey with me.

Next Steps

So, you've read the book and you're compelled to move forward. You're ready for your next steps. Here are some ways we can support you on your journey:

Walking With My Angels: A True Story soft cover book

Walking With My Angels Kindle Book

Walking With My Angels Audio Book

Walking With Your Angels Vision Deck

Walking With Your Angels Greeting Cards

Walking With Your Angels Companion Workbook

Walking With Your Angels Evocations & Meditations

Walking With Your Angels Home Study Course

Walking With Your Angels Group Mentor Course

For those who want to write a book:

Bake Your Book Home Study Writing Course
(When you order the Home Study Course -
Enter Coupon Code: ANGEL)

To order your support programs and products, go to:
www.BeyondBeliefBooks.com

Special Offers:

Let's Keep You Writing Facebook Support Group
Purchase Here: http://tinyurl.com/BYBwrite

YouSpeakIt Book Program
Purchase Here: http://tinyurl.com/WWMAspecial

Personal Mentoring with Keith Leon S.
Purchase Here: http://tinyurl.com/KeithLeonS

Read full description of these programs at:
www.BeyondBeliefBooks.com

To book Keith Leon S. to speak at your next event!
Contact Keith Leon S. via email at: keith@bakeyourbook.com

About the Author

Keith Leon is a multiple best-selling author, publisher, and book mentor, and has become well known as *The Book Guy*. With his wife, Maura, Keith authored the book, *The Seven Steps to Successful Relationships,* acclaimed by best-selling authors John Gray and Terry Cole-Whittaker, and Keith authored the best-selling book *Who Do You Think You Are? Discover the Purpose of Your Life,* with a foreword by *Chicken Soup for The Soul's* Jack Canfield.

Keith's writing has also been featured in Warren Henningsen's *If I Can You Can,* Jennifer McLean's *The Big Book of You,* Justin Sachs' *The Power of Persistence,* Ronny K. Prasad's *Welcome To Your Life,* Anton Uhl's *Feeding Body, Mind and Soul,* Bardi Toto's, *Thinking Upside Down Living Rightside Up,* Keith Leon and Maribel Jimenez' *The Bake Your Book Program: How to Finish Your Book Fast and Serve it Up HOT, PIVOT: The Art and Science of Reinventing Your Life,* by Adam Markel, and many other books, including Keith's latest bestseller, *YOU Make a Difference: 50 Heart-Centered Entrepreneurs Share Their Stories of Inspiration and Transformation.*

Keith has appeared on popular radio and television broadcasts, including *The Rolonda Watts Show* and *The John Kerwin Show*, and his work has been covered by *Inc. Magazine, Published Magazine, LA Weekly, The Valley Reporter, The Minneapolis-St. Paul Star Tribune, The Maryland Herald-Mail, The Huffington Post* and *Succeed Magazine* just to name a few.

As a professional speaker, Keith has spoken at events that included Jack Canfield, Dr. John Demartini, Neale Donald Walsch, Joel Bauer, Armand Morin, Brian Tracy, Bob Proctor, Paul Martinelli, Barbara De Angelis, Dr. John Gray, Dr. Michael Beckwith, Alex Mandossian, T. Harv Eker, Adam Markel, and Marianne Williamson.

Keith is a long-time member of Agape, an Agape International Choir member, and a singer/songwriter who has made music with Stevie Wonder, Ben Vereen, Nancy Wilson, Carl Anderson, Gloria Loring, Keb' Mo' and The Wood Brothers.

Keith's passion is teaching people how to go from first thought to bestseller, and showing them how to manifest the life of their dreams. He does this through personal mentoring, ghost writing services, and home-study courses. His company, Leon Smith Publishing, offers any book services you may need to get your book out to the world.

Find out more about Keith at www.LeonSmithPublishing.com